Devoted Money

-

A Monday Morning Devotional

by
Travis T Pugh

An Ashar Media Publication

Cover photography by Joshua Pugh

"Scripture taken from the NEW AMERICAN STANDARD BIBLE®, Copyright © 1960,1962,1963,1968,1971,1972,1973,1975,1977,1995 by The Lockman Foundation. Used by permission."
Scripture taken from New American Standard Bible marked as (NASB)

Scripture taken from the New King James Version®. Copyright © 1982 by Thomas Nelson. Used by permission. All rights reserved.
Scripture taken from New King James Version marked as (NKJV)

Scripture quotations are taken from the *Holy Bible*, New Living Translation, copyright © 1996, 2004, 2015 by Tyndale House Foundation. Used by permission of Tyndale House Publishers, Inc., Carol Stream, Illinois 60188. All rights reserved.
Scripture taken from the New Living Translation marked as (NLT)

Scripture taken from the King James Version are marked as (KJV) and are public domain in the United States.

Scripture quotations marked HCSB are taken from the Holman Christian Standard Bible®, Copyright © 1999, 2000, 2002, 2003, 2009 by Holman Bible Publishers. Used by permission. Holman Christian Standard Bible®, Holman CSB®, and HCSB® are federally registered trademarks of Holman Bible Publishers.

Scripture quotations marked CSB are taken from the Christian Standard Bible®, Copyright © 2017 by Holman Bible Publishers. Used by permission. Christian Standard Bible® and CSB® are federally registered trademarks of Holman Bible Publishers.

Scripture is taken from GOD'S WORD®, © 1995 God's Word to the Nations. Used by permission of Baker Publishing Group.
Scripture taken from the God's Word Translation marked as (GWT)

New Revised Standard Version Bible, copyright © 1989 the Division of Christian Education of the National Council of the Churches of Christ in the United States of America. Used by permission. All rights reserved.
Scripture taken from the New Revised Standard Version Bible marked as (NRSV)

Scripture quotations marked (ESV) are taken from The ESV® Bible (The Holy Bible, English Standard Version. ESV® Text Edition: 2016. Copyright © 2001 by Crossway Bibles, a publishing ministry of Good News Publishers. Used by permission. All rights reserved.

Scripture quotations marked (AMPC) are taken from the Amplified® Bible (AMPC), Copyright © 1954, 1958, 1962, 1964, 1965, 1987 by The Lockman Foundation Used by permission. www.Lockman.org"

Scripture quotations marked (GNT) are taken from the Good News Translation in Today's English Version-Second Edition Copyright © 1992 by American Bible Society. Used by Permission.

Scripture quotations marked (MEV) are taken from the Modern English Version. Copyright © 2014 by Military Bible Association. Used by permission. All rights reserved.

Scripture quotations mark (NIV) are taken from THE HOLY BIBLE, NEW INTERNATIONAL VERSION®, NIV® Copyright © 1973, 1978, 1984, 2011 by Biblica, Inc.™ Used by permission. All rights reserved worldwide.

Devoted Money-A Monday Morning Devotional ©2020
Cover photography by Joshua Pugh

Contents

Devoted Money – a Monday Morning Devotional

Testify	5
Introduction	7
Example	8

Week 1	9	Week 27	113
Week 2	13	Week 28	117
Week 3	17	Week 29	121
Week 4	21	Week 30	125
Week 5	25	Week 31	129
Week 6	29	Week 32	133
Week 7	33	Week 33	137
Week 8	37	Week 34	141
Week 9	41	Week 35	145
Week 10	45	Week 36	149
Week 11	49	Week 37	153
Week 12	53	Week 38	157
Week 13	57	Week 39	161
Week 14	61	Week 40	165
Week 15	65	Week 41	169
Week 16	69	Week 42	173
Week 17	73	Week 43	177
Week 18	77	Week 44	181
Week 19	81	Week 45	185
Week 20	85	Week 46	189
Week 21	89	Week 47	193
Week 22	93	Week 48	197
Week 23	97	Week 49	201
Week 24	101	Week 50	205
Week 25	105	Week 51	209
Week 26	109	Week 52	213

A Parting Prayer	219
The Heart of the Matter	221
Our Hope and Salvation	223

Thank you,
    to all who helped make this devotional.

Editors -   Micah Pugh,
                     Joshua Pugh,
                     Henrietta Pugh

Content Editor -   Kathy Battles

First, all Glory be to the Father...

I will be telling many of my testimonies about the Goodness of God in the financial realm. I will tell many times of how God would move on my heart to help people with money. I would like to take a moment here to make sure all glory for any such things goes to my Father.

I grew up in western Oklahoma during the oil bust. I saw what having no money does. I saw people lose houses; I saw them come and take our car away. I knew what it was not to be able to have the right clothes. I knew what it was not to be able to go to a movie theater or have any video games (this does not make having friends easy). I knew what it was to eat bread and ketchup sandwiches. I saw all those final notices, and I saw the wires sticking out of the car tires.

These things did something awful to my heart. I valued money, I way overvalued money. I would not eat lunch at school, so I could have that dollar bill. I knew the cost of not having money, so I held onto it at all costs.

I was also a Christian, and I knew that I had to give. I was sure that if I didn't give God would surely make me pay. I knew how to trust God for my salvation and my health, but in the realm of money; I was on my own.

As I entered adulthood and joined the working world; I paid God what I had to when I had to, but then I had to make all the numbers work.

My heart was truly awful. I would give but I never *wanted to*. I never had any joy or peace about giving. I was always counting the cost and running those numbers.

Then one day at church a visiting missionary came. He told of his wonderful ministry and of all the good works of God that were happening. I was overjoyed and so excited for him and the Kingdom. And then... They took up an offering. I was shocked and appalled at my own evil heart's reaction. "I have already paid what I owe."

God told me that day not to give any more, period. Well, that violated my religion. But over the next many months, with the pressure of 'have to' lifted, God began to work on my heart. Soon thereafter God began to have me cross paths with ministers and ministries, that I truly loved. I found myself asking God to please lift His ban on my giving, and let me be a help to the Kingdom. God had begun a good work in my heart and He continues it to this day. I am amazed many times at the things He has me do, but I am more amazed at the change in my heart. He is my Lord, and He is my God. I love Him dearly for changing those awful, evil things inside of me. God forever will receive the glory and the honor for any good that it appears I may have done.

So, as I tell these testimonies please remember it wasn't me. I was the man in Proverbs 23...

⁶ DON'T EAT WITH PEOPLE WHO ARE STINGY; DON'T DESIRE THEIR DELICACIES.
⁷ THEY ARE ALWAYS THINKING ABOUT HOW MUCH IT COSTS. "EAT AND DRINK," THEY SAY, BUT THEY DON'T MEAN IT.
Proverbs 23:6-8 (NLT)

Selfish, self-centered,
and completely devoid of faith in God in these things.
But God...

Now I find myself chasing after opportunities to give. I still don't really understand when I receive a thank you, for such things; it's really not me. My Father did this, He is the one responsible, and He should have the acknowledgment and acclaim. I am just so full of peace and joy, that He took out my old, cold, evil, heart and gave me a new one that reminds me of His.

Thank you Papa, I love you dearly.

Introduction...

The devotions of this book are taken from the "Devoted Money" radio devotional. This study is meant to turn our eyes to our Father and His Word concerning our money and finances. Monday mornings are, for most of us, the start of our working week. I hope this devotional will help us to consider God, His Word, and His ways as we begin our week. In no way is this meant to be a confining restriction on when, where, and how to walk through this devotional.

First there will be a devotion, and then I will share a testimony. I then invite and encourage the reader to set pen to page and share as well. I would encourage the reader, now writer, to pause for a moment and allow the Spirit to reveal this testimony. I personally did not think that I had more than a dozen or so financial testimonies from my nearly 40 years of walking with the Lord. Then the Holy Spirit started to show and reveal the Hand of God over this area of my walk. He showed, revealed, and reminded me of all the testimonies written here, in one night. So, I challenge you to let Him show you, that you may be encouraged and inspired by all the great and small things which God has done. I would also remind and encourage the reader to take His Word by faith. Don't let discouragement, fear, or condemnation have any place in your heart as you read His great and precious promises. It matters little what our life looks like, or what seems to have always been. What matters is His Word, His promises, and His plans and purposes.
I hope and pray you will receive, by faith, all that the Father has for you.

I have also left space to write a prayer for the week, the month, or the season of life. I hope we can step away from religious tradition and simply speak to our Father about these matters that do so tend to press upon us daily.

Next, I left another space for the reader to prophesy. I understand that you may not stand in the office of the prophet, but you can prophesy over yourself, your life, your family, and your finances. We are in the image of our Father; we do speak words of faith and they will manifest in this present world. I hope and pray with all that is in me, that these prophesies are based upon Him, and His Word. Let us endeavor to cast off tradition, resist convention, hold back the pressure of circumstances; let us simply, plainly, boldly speak the Words of our good, Good Father (The Almighty God).

And finally, there's scripture for us to consider throughout the week.

Addendum: I normally prefer not to use numbers in giving of testimonies, but as this is a devotion specifically about money, finances, and blessings; I will tell actual numbers. I simply pray this will help us to see that God handles all things well, small things and not quite so small things. God, His Blessing, and His Abundance do not change, no matter how big or small the matter.

Example...

Testify...

One afternoon, the Lord reminded me of a debt I owed to a friend. He had picked up some parts for me and I had not repaid him. It wasn't a massive amount so I didn't think much of it. Of course, I would repay the debt but at a convenient time for us both. When the Lord brought it up, my mind was ready to dismiss it as no big deal (I'll take care of it soon enough). But my spirit knew better, if God is bringing it up, it is a big deal. So, I called my friend and brought him the money that afternoon. He then told me that he had been praying to the Lord about money. He had a mortgage payment due, but it would not leave hardly any money for about a week until he got paid again. His natural mind was telling him to pay the mortgage late, so he could make it to his next check. His spirit was telling him to make that payment, so he had brought the matter to the Lord that morning. The money I brought him took the pressure off his situation and was an answer to his prayer. (Obedience and timely obedience are important in the kingdom.)

Pray...

Father, we pray that we hear you clearly and obey you quickly. We pray that the Spirit would give us ears to hear and the grace to walk in obedience all of our days.

Prophesy...

We are the blessed of the Lord and all that we set our hands to will prosper as we walk with Him, this day and every day.

Week #1
Good Morning, today we will be reading **Deuteronomy 28:1-14** (HCSB)

"Now if you faithfully obey the Lord your God and are careful to follow all His commands I am giving you today, the Lord your God will put you far above all the nations of the earth. 2 All these blessings will come and overtake you, because you obey the Lord your God:

3 You will be blessed in the city and blessed in the country. 4 Your descendants will be blessed, and your land's produce, and the offspring of your livestock, including the young of your herds and the newborn of your flocks. 5 Your basket and kneading bowl will be blessed. 6 You will be blessed when you come in and blessed when you go out.

7 "The Lord will cause the enemies who rise up against you to be defeated before you. They will march out against you from one direction but flee from you in seven directions. 8 The Lord will grant you a blessing on your storehouses and on everything you do; He will bless you in the land the Lord your God is giving you. 9 The Lord will establish you as His holy people, as He swore to you, if you obey the commands of the Lord your God and walk in His ways. 10 Then all the peoples of the earth will see that you are called by Yahweh's name, and they will stand in awe of you. 11 The Lord will make you prosper abundantly with children, the offspring of your livestock, and your land's produce in the land the Lord swore to your fathers to give you. 12 The Lord will open for you His abundant storehouse, the sky, to give your land rain in its season and to bless all the work of your hands. You will lend to many nations, but you will not borrow. 13 The Lord will make you the head and not the tail; you will only move upward and never downward if you listen to the Lord your God's commands I am giving you today and are careful to follow them. 14 Do not turn aside to the right or the left from all the things I am commanding you today, and do not go after other gods to worship them.

I hope that here we can see the good nature of God. His primary concern is for our spiritual (eternal) wellbeing. Obey and walk with Him, this is the command. Once the primary is addressed now the secondary; blessing, abundance, and wealth; can be addressed. God wants to bless His children with abundance. He wants us to walk with Him, and as we do, He is free to pour out blessings that we cannot contain.

We pray the Lord bless you, today.

A Testimony....

For several years we had saved and planned for projected building projects on our small farm. (We lived far away from the farm due to my wife's work.) Then the time came that we would have one year to go and stay at the farm and complete these projects. We had made a very detailed budget and a specific timeline.

But then, just as we arrived at the farm, we heard about a dear sister in the Lord who was about to be sued over medical bills. The hospital had been sold and by the time the new company processed her bill, it was overdue and sent to collections. She did not in any way have the ability to pay the bill, all at once and in full. Now, they were threatening to add collection fees, attorney fees, and court costs.

The Lord told us to give her more than enough to cover everything. We told her she could repay, what she could when she could.

(We should never let Kingdom children be threatened and oppressed by a financial matter; when God has blessed us to be able to help and the Holy Spirit leads us to be a blessing. "Don't mess with God's kids, (He is a mighty God, and well able to deliver) don't mess with our brothers and sisters, this is one body.")

Ok, the numbers...

We had saved $20,000 for our farm projects. Now before we even started, we had just given away $5000. I am a real numbers kind of person; I like the certainty of mathematics. So, if you give away a quarter of your budget, then you have to cut back a quarter of your projects, right? God, over and over that year, told me not to readjust my budget and not to cut back on any projects.

We had expected, before helping our sister, that at the end of that year we would have all the projects done and all the money spent. It was the trade we agreed to in the budget, money goes out and buildings go up. Well, with no money raining down from the sky and no gold bars popping out of the ground, we got all of our projects done that year. Everything we wanted to do was completed, we even hired a family member to work for us for some months. And when the year was done and the projects finished, we did not have $0.00 in the bank. It would have been a great thing to be able to help someone and still complete all those projects with a quarter of the budget missing. **But God...** At the end of that year, the account had $20,000. I do have a degree in Mathematics, and I just can't explain it with simple pluses and minuses. **But God...**

Testify...

_____
_____
_____
_____
_____
_____
_____

Pray...

_____
_____
_____
_____
_____
_____
_____

Prophesy...

_____
_____
_____
_____
_____

"The

LORD

Bless

you...

Numbers 6:24a (NKJV)

Week #2

Good Morning, today we will be reading 3 John 1:2 (NASB).

Beloved, I pray that in all respects you may prosper and be in good health, just as your soul prospers.

And 3 John 1:2 (KJV)

Beloved, I wish above all things that thou mayest prosper and be in health, even as thy soul prospereth.

And finally, 3 John 1:2 (HCSB)

Dear friend, I pray that you may prosper in every way and be in good health physically just as you are spiritually.

Here we see that God is interested in all of you and all aspects of your life. God knows you; He made you (all the parts of you). He knows where, when, and how you live. He wants and desires to bless you. Truly, spiritual matters are of preeminence. As we walk with God and He develops us spiritually, we need to allow Him access to all areas of our life. He wants to prosper you in *all* areas. He wants you to do well in your career. He wants you to do well in your relationships. And He wants you to do well in your kingdom work. Our Father is a GOOD Father and He wants to bless. The greatest, most valuable, and eternal things will always be spiritual. But your God, the almighty God, can and will bless you financially. He loves to bless His kids; it gives Him great joy.

We pray the Lord bless you, today.

A Testimony....

I have a very good friend who is an accomplished man of God, who also happens to be 20 years my senior. One day I happened to meet him in passing, which was kind of odd as we live miles apart in different towns. I could tell something was weighing on him, so I suggested we go to lunch. At lunch, he told me that he was headed to the bank to try and get a loan against his vehicle. He had needed to travel across the country several times in the last several months for "the right thing to do" moments (family and funerals). He was retired and living on a fixed income. He simply could not pay all these incurred expenses at once. He reluctantly told me the amount was $2,000. I asked him if I could just loan him the money. He was hesitant and explained it could take a while to repay. I actually had to bring up scripture to convince him.

IF SOMEONE HAS ENOUGH MONEY TO LIVE WELL AND SEES A BROTHER OR SISTER IN NEED BUT SHOWS NO COMPASSION—HOW CAN GOD'S LOVE BE IN THAT PERSON?
1 John 3:17 (NLT)

I made the case that I must (driven by compassion) do everything I can to help my brother. So, to keep me out of trouble he agreed. Then he insisted on repaying me with interest, and again we had to go to scriptures.

"DO NOT CHARGE YOUR BROTHER INTEREST ON MONEY, FOOD, OR ANYTHING THAT CAN EARN INTEREST.
Deuteronomy 23:19 (HCSB)

So finally, we agree to simple terms. Our friendship deepened that day as we walked together as brothers in the Body of Christ. We not only talked and reasoned the holy scriptures, but we lived them.

Testify...

Pray...

Prophesy...

...and

(the LORD)

Keep

you;

Numbers 6:24b (NKJV)

Week #3

Good Morning, today we will be reading **Deuteronomy 30:8-10**(NASB).

8 AND YOU SHALL AGAIN OBEY THE LORD, AND OBSERVE ALL HIS COMMANDMENTS WHICH I COMMAND YOU TODAY. 9 THEN THE LORD YOUR GOD WILL PROSPER YOU ABUNDANTLY IN ALL THE WORK OF YOUR HAND, IN THE OFFSPRING OF YOUR BODY AND IN THE OFFSPRING OF YOUR CATTLE AND IN THE PRODUCE OF YOUR GROUND, FOR THE LORD WILL AGAIN REJOICE OVER YOU FOR GOOD, JUST AS HE REJOICED OVER YOUR FATHERS; 10 IF YOU OBEY THE LORD YOUR GOD TO KEEP HIS COMMANDMENTS AND HIS STATUTES WHICH ARE WRITTEN IN THIS BOOK OF THE LAW, IF YOU TURN TO THE LORD YOUR GOD WITH ALL YOUR HEART AND SOUL.

Look at our Father's heart at the end of verse 9;

"…rejoice over you for good…"

Let us read verse 9 in the Holman Christian Standard Bible.

THE LORD YOUR GOD WILL MAKE YOU PROSPER ABUNDANTLY IN ALL THE WORK OF YOUR HANDS WITH CHILDREN, THE OFFSPRING OF YOUR LIVESTOCK, AND YOUR LAND'S PRODUCE. INDEED, THE LORD WILL AGAIN DELIGHT IN YOUR PROSPERITY, AS HE DELIGHTED IN THAT OF YOUR FATHERS,

Deuteronomy 30:9 (HCSB)

He delights in your prosperity.

We also want our children to do well. We rejoice when they do well in school. We rejoice when they find a good career. We are overjoyed when they themselves have children. These traits did not come from our nature, but from our heavenly Father.

And remember this passage was written to those who had strayed from God and then returned. God was not holding grudges, or reducing them to 'less than.' He was ready to forgive, restore, and bless His children.

We pray the Lord bless you, today.

A Testimony....

Years ago, a friend of mine from church asked me to come with him to check out a vehicle he wanted to buy. His car had been hit by another vehicle and totaled out. That was his only car so he needed a vehicle. The insurance company had paid him the value of his old car. He had found a small SUV and was really excited about it. So, we went to the dealer, looked it over, and went for a test drive. He decided to purchase the SUV, but the payout from the insurance company was not enough. He was a young man just starting out in life; so, he didn't have any extra money and no credit. I could see how nervous he was, as the salesman went to get the paperwork for a loan. All he needed was $500; which in my world was a small thing, but in his, it was a huge mountain. I asked him if I could just loan him the money. This young man, a big guy, began to well up with tears in the middle of the car dealership. (*Money used correctly can demonstrate love and can really help people.*) We got everything settled and my friend got his vehicle. Lots of things got disrupted in the accident. How could he get to work and church? Would he be able to go home to see his family for the holidays? A lot of peace came when this was finally settled, and it didn't hurt that he liked the vehicle.

Later, after many more bumps in the road for this young man, the Lord told me to cancel the rest of the loan repayment after the young man made one payment. (It was a struggle for him, and no small act of faith to keep his word and make that payment.) When he handed me the payment, I told him that God said the loan was repaid in full. I saw the relief in his eyes and saw the weight fall off his shoulders. (*When we are led by God's Spirit, we can do good things with money.*)

It is always amazing to me how money and the simple act of being generous can so show people the love and kindness of God. It is also beyond my comprehension, that God would take my family (coming from such meager and humble beginnings) to a place where we are so blessed that we can be a blessing.

Testify...

_____
_____
_____
_____
_____
_____

Pray...

_____
_____
_____
_____
_____
_____

Prophesy...

_____
_____
_____
_____
_____

The LORD make His face shine upon you,

Numbers 6:25a (NKJV)

Week #4

Good Morning, today we will be reading Matthew 7:1-2 (KJV).

¹JUDGE NOT, THAT YE BE NOT JUDGED. ²FOR WITH WHAT JUDGMENT YE JUDGE, YE SHALL BE JUDGED: AND WITH WHAT MEASURE YE METE, IT SHALL BE MEASURED TO YOU AGAIN.

Walking with the Lord is like walking down a path. In the center of the path, things are pretty well smooth and easy to travel. But the more you drift away from the center of that path the bumpier and rockier things get. You can eventually find yourself off the path completely, and stuck in a ditch. Remember there are ditches on either side. As we study the kingdom principles of blessings, prosperity, and money; we also need to be aware of the various ditches.

Today, we will look at judgment. We need to be aware of the perils of judging people based on their level of prosperity. Can the one who drives a BMW, judge the one driving a Ferrari because that is too excessive? Can the one who drives a Chevy, judge the one driving a Cadillac? Can they all be judged by all those millions of people on this planet who only have two motorized wheels instead of four? Or can *those* millions be judged by the 10's of millions on this planet that only have two wheels and two pedals to move them along?

Judgment is tricky and best left to our Father.

Remember ~ **Romans 14:4 (KJV)**
⁴ WHO ART THOU THAT JUDGEST ANOTHER MAN'S SERVANT? TO HIS OWN MASTER HE STANDETH OR FALLETH. YEA, HE SHALL BE HOLDEN UP: FOR GOD IS ABLE TO MAKE HIM STAND.

Let us endeavor to learn the kingdom principles of blessings and abundance. But let us not use our knowledge to tear apart our brethren. Let us not judge who has too much, or too little. We don't judge the brother or sister who has tremendous abundance. God may have appointed them to be a great blessing to his people and the kingdom. Even if greed or self-sufficiency has entered their heart, let God correct and lead them.

Let us also never judge a brother or sister who is struggling to walk in the blessings of God and accuse them of not having faith, or knowledge of the blessing. We do not know their giftings, their callings, or their faith. Let us never be an 'accuser of the brethren'; we do not play for that team.

We love our God, and as He loves people, so do we. We will bless the kingdom and our dear brothers and sisters. We will help our neighbors. We will build and not tear down. Thank you, Father, for keeping our hearts tender toward our brothers and sisters.

We pray the Lord bless you, today.

A Testimony....

I was talking to a brother in the Lord and he told me that he was saving money and trusting God to buy a new guitar. This brother had been saved and delivered from a completely derailed life. He was walking with God mightily, but finances were still a struggle to rebuild. As we were talking, my heart ignited, I eagerly and excitedly wanted to help him get this guitar (*again this in and of itself is a miracle, considering my original nature*). I simply did not have any money with me and I felt a check in my spirit, so I knew I needed to talk to God about this. My brother needed $500 to buy this dream guitar. He had seen it in a music store and was actually going to drive thirty minutes just to go see it again the day he told me about it.

I went to God and asked if I could give my brother the $500. But God said to give him $250. I was not happy, and I argued with God for several days. I got really confused by all this, I just couldn't understand why God would not let me give my brother all he needed. So, I went to my pastor for help and he gave me the same words that I had just told my own children about walking with God. He said, "What did God tell you to do?" The simplicity of Truth, evaporated all my high arguments. So, I gave my brother the $250.

At the next church service, I saw that he had a new guitar. After service, he came and told me the tale. He had gone back to the music store to see and play the guitar he wanted. While there he saw a new guitar that had just arrived. He played it and liked it more than the original one. And guess how much that guitar cost... $250. He left that day with his new guitar, which played better and was half the price.

God is God, and we simply are not. Let Him arrange this life, let Him work out the details, and let Him always be in control of all things; especially our money. He can make all things work for the good, and only He can make all things work, **well**.

Testify...

_____
_____
_____
_____
_____
_____

Pray...

_____
_____
_____
_____
_____
_____

Prophesy...

_____
_____
_____
_____
_____

And

(the LORD)

be gracious

to you;

Numbers 6:25b (NKJV)

Week #5

Good Morning, today we will be reading **Genesis 13:5-15** (NKJV).

5 LOT ALSO, WHO WENT WITH ABRAM, HAD FLOCKS AND HERDS AND TENTS. 6 NOW THE LAND WAS NOT ABLE TO SUPPORT THEM, THAT THEY MIGHT DWELL TOGETHER, FOR THEIR POSSESSIONS WERE SO GREAT THAT THEY COULD NOT DWELL TOGETHER. 7 AND THERE WAS STRIFE BETWEEN THE HERDSMEN OF ABRAM'S LIVESTOCK AND THE HERDSMEN OF LOT'S LIVESTOCK. THE CANAANITES AND THE PERIZZITES THEN DWELT IN THE LAND.

8 SO ABRAM SAID TO LOT, "PLEASE LET THERE BE NO STRIFE BETWEEN YOU AND ME, AND BETWEEN MY HERDSMEN AND YOUR HERDSMEN; FOR WE ARE BRETHREN. 9 IS NOT THE WHOLE LAND BEFORE YOU? PLEASE SEPARATE FROM ME. IF YOU TAKE THE LEFT, THEN I WILL GO TO THE RIGHT; OR, IF YOU GO TO THE RIGHT, THEN I WILL GO TO THE LEFT."

10 AND LOT LIFTED HIS EYES AND SAW ALL THE PLAIN OF JORDAN, THAT IT WAS WELL WATERED EVERYWHERE (BEFORE THE LORD DESTROYED SODOM AND GOMORRAH) LIKE THE GARDEN OF THE LORD, LIKE THE LAND OF EGYPT AS YOU GO TOWARD ZOAR. 11 THEN LOT CHOSE FOR HIMSELF ALL THE PLAIN OF JORDAN, AND LOT JOURNEYED EAST. AND THEY SEPARATED FROM EACH OTHER. 12 ABRAM DWELT IN THE LAND OF CANAAN, AND LOT DWELT IN THE CITIES OF THE PLAIN AND PITCHED HIS TENT EVEN AS FAR AS SODOM. 13 BUT THE MEN OF SODOM WERE EXCEEDINGLY WICKED AND SINFUL AGAINST THE LORD.

14 AND THE LORD SAID TO ABRAM, AFTER LOT HAD SEPARATED FROM HIM: "LIFT YOUR EYES NOW AND LOOK FROM THE PLACE WHERE YOU ARE—NORTHWARD, SOUTHWARD, EASTWARD, AND WESTWARD; 15 FOR ALL THE LAND WHICH YOU SEE I GIVE TO YOU AND YOUR DESCENDANTS FOREVER.

How could Abram (the senior) give Lot (the junior) first choice? Lot took the best-looking land. Abram should have gotten the best land, shouldn't he?

Abram (Abraham) knew that being with God was the key to the blessing, not annual rainfall or soil conditions. Strife was the dangerous thing, not right or left. With God, it doesn't matter whether you are in New York or New Guinea. With God, it doesn't matter how many college degrees you have. With God, it doesn't matter if the world is in a slowdown, a correction, or a recession. We have God, blessings abound in Him. Abram left everything in Haran because He believed that God was good, and would fulfill all those good promises. Life with God is good. The issue is never our education, our career, or our nationality. The only question for us is, are we walking close with our Father? Can we believe? Can we leave all? He is waiting to take that walk with us... He is waiting to pour out all those blessings upon His dear children...

We pray the Lord bless you, today.

A Testimony....

One day I was on my way to pick up some septic pipe for a new project on our farm. I had planned out all the details of the day. It was about an hour and a half drive to pick up the pipe. I checked the store's inventory online and set out for the day. I planned to go out to pick up the pipe, then go by a farm supply store, and then on the way home stop at the bank. I needed to go by the bank to get $250 to give to my brother in the Lord for his guitar (see last week's testimony). I may just be a little obsessive-compulsive so plans and details are usually important to me. As we set out (my mother had joined me) the Lord told me to go to the bank, first. God had just been teaching me about putting the kingdom first, so I knew it was the right thing to do, but... I had made all my plans. I had everything set in order. I did obey Him, but I sure was not happy about it. I even clocked the delay, seven minutes. (Now I had all day, and everything should have taken 5-6 hours, so I did have time.) I was smiling on the outside, but in my mind, I was really upset about Him turning my plans upside down.

Then we arrived at the store to pick up the pipe, but they didn't have any. Now, my day was really ruined. I had checked the online inventory, but it was for another location that I go to. It had over 50 sticks of pipe, and I only needed 10. I just reasoned that if that location had 50, the other would at least have 10. But they had nothing. I had hooked up the trailer, driven all that way, and now I have lost the day. I wasn't even smiling on the outside now. We left the store and headed to the farm supply store. My mom asked if we could get the pipe there. I told her they didn't keep it in stock (in all my years of shopping there I had never seen septic pipe). When we arrived, there was a large pile of pipe laying out in their side yard. Again, my mom asked about it. I was explaining that it was the wrong kind of pipe, as we walked toward the door. An employee from out in the yard asked if we were interested in the pipe, and said the boss had told him just to get rid of it. He offered all that pipe for the price of one stick; $15. Well, I just had to come around and look. At the bottom of the pile was all the septic pipe I needed and more. We bought the whole lot (worth $400) for $15. I got everything I needed for my project and several other projects.

I could then, finally see the day. God had arranged that day, and He needed to delay my schedule by those seven minutes. If that employee had not been out in that side yard at the exact time we were walking by and talking about the pipe, he would not have made the offer. I would have never gone to see what was in the pile, and my day would have been empty.

First things first, then all things work together for good.
Also, it was a cool blessing that before I even actually gave the gift, I had received an even greater blessing.

Testify...

_____
_____
_____
_____
_____
_____
_____

Pray...

_____
_____
_____
_____
_____
_____
_____

Prophesy...

_____
_____
_____
_____
_____

The LORD lift up His countenance upon you,

Numbers 6:26a (NKJV)

Week #6

Good Morning, today we will be reading **Genesis 26:1-5** (NKJV).

¹ THERE WAS A FAMINE IN THE LAND, BESIDES THE FIRST FAMINE THAT WAS IN THE DAYS OF ABRAHAM. AND ISAAC WENT TO ABIMELECH KING OF THE PHILISTINES, IN GERAR. ² THEN THE LORD APPEARED TO HIM AND SAID: "DO NOT GO DOWN TO EGYPT; LIVE IN THE LAND OF WHICH I SHALL TELL YOU. ³ DWELL IN THIS LAND, AND I WILL BE WITH YOU AND BLESS YOU; FOR TO YOU AND YOUR DESCENDANTS I GIVE ALL THESE LANDS, AND I WILL PERFORM THE OATH WHICH I SWORE TO ABRAHAM YOUR FATHER. ⁴ AND I WILL MAKE YOUR DESCENDANTS MULTIPLY AS THE STARS OF HEAVEN; I WILL GIVE TO YOUR DESCENDANTS ALL THESE LANDS; AND IN YOUR SEED ALL THE NATIONS OF THE EARTH SHALL BE BLESSED; ⁵ BECAUSE ABRAHAM OBEYED MY VOICE AND KEPT MY CHARGE, MY COMMANDMENTS, MY STATUTES, AND MY LAWS."

There was a famine in the land... Logic says go to Egypt; reason says you will suffer loss if you stay in this land. Do we know our God well enough, to defy logic and reason? Do we have faith in His Goodness? Will He save us, protect us, and bless us, or do we need to run to Egypt? Let's see what Isaac, the son of Abraham (the father of faith) did? **Genesis 26:12-16** (NKJV)

¹² THEN ISAAC SOWED IN THAT LAND, AND REAPED IN THE SAME YEAR A HUNDREDFOLD; AND THE LORD BLESSED HIM. ¹³ THE MAN BEGAN TO PROSPER, AND CONTINUED PROSPERING UNTIL HE BECAME VERY PROSPEROUS; ¹⁴ FOR HE HAD POSSESSIONS OF FLOCKS AND POSSESSIONS OF HERDS AND A GREAT NUMBER OF SERVANTS. SO THE PHILISTINES ENVIED HIM. ¹⁵ NOW THE PHILISTINES HAD STOPPED UP ALL THE WELLS WHICH HIS FATHER'S SERVANTS HAD DUG IN THE DAYS OF ABRAHAM HIS FATHER, AND THEY HAD FILLED THEM WITH EARTH. ¹⁶ AND ABIMELECH SAID TO ISAAC, "GO AWAY FROM US, FOR YOU ARE MUCH MIGHTIER THAN WE."

I know those words "hundredfold" and "very prosperous" seem dangerous, but here we have the son of Abraham (the father of our faith) obeying God, and abiding with God. Not relying on reason, logic, or religion, and God blessed him.

We pray the Lord bless you, today.

A Testimony....

When we purchased our farm, we had been so amazingly blessed by God that we were able to buy it outright. We were simply able to bring a cashier's check to closing. I was really overwhelmed by the goodness of God, and I simply asked Him, "How and why did this happen?" Financially, mathematically, and culturally there was just no way for this to happen. Then God showed me something that happened about 5 years previous.

My family was moving to Japan for my wife's work. I would be quitting my job to move. So, our income was literally getting cut in half. We had a one-year-old and a four-year-old, who had been going to their grandmother's daycare. We had decided that I would stay at home with them in Japan. So again, our income was about to be cut in half and we were moving just outside of Tokyo, one of the most expensive cities on the planet.

Our family had developed in giving and it had grown to no small amount relative to our income. For weeks; logic, reason, mathematics, and budgets were really pressing on us to stop all our giving. Just to stop everything until we got settled. Just stop until we knew how everything would work on the other side of the planet. Just stop until the budget and the math said it was ok to start giving again. Then from somewhere deep in my heart, I cried out. No, we would not stop giving. We would in fact increase our giving right then.

(Again, this is the amazing transforming power of God. He had changed my heart from "have to" give. He gave me a love for the people and His Kingdom. Love, simply would not quit. Love simply would not be bullied by fear of the known. Love would not submit to logic, reason, math, or budgets.)

God blessed us beyond measure while in Japan. We did not suffer loss as we gave but we walked in "more than enough". Then over five years later and back again in the United States, we were in overflowing abundance. God showed me that making that choice to trust Him, opened the door for Him to bless our family. To value the Kingdom and others over ourselves allows Him to bless us far beyond all that logic, reason, budget, position, location, and mathematics could account for.

Thank you, Father. You are so good to us. We love you, always.

Testify...

___

Pray...

___

Prophesy...

___

And
(the LORD)
give you
peace."

Numbers 6:26b (NKJV)

Week #7

Good Morning, today we will be reading **2 Corinthians 9:7** (KNJV).

So let each one give as he purposes in his heart, not grudgingly or of necessity; for God loves a cheerful giver.

And **2 Corinthians 9:7** (NLT) reads

You must each decide in your heart how much to give. And don't give reluctantly or in response to pressure. "For God loves a person who gives cheerfully."

And **2 Corinthians 9:7** (GNT) reads

You should each give, then, as you have decided, not with regret or out of a sense of duty; for God loves the one who gives gladly.

And finally, **2 Corinthians 9:7** (GW) reads

Each of you should give whatever you have decided. You shouldn't be sorry that you gave or feel forced to give, since God loves a cheerful giver

Okay, but why? Isn't giving a good thing to do, isn't it the right thing to do? Why does how I "feel" about it make any difference? Shouldn't I do what is right, even if I don't feel cheerful about it?

If we give out from a place of "have to" then we show our limited faith and understanding of our Father. We 'have to' or God won't like us anymore. We 'have to' or God will drop that big hammer we think He always has hanging over our head. Others may pressure us to give, and even our own religious beliefs will pressure us to give, but our Father never will. Make no mistake, God wants us to give, but not unless it comes from a place of faith. When we know God loves us and has taken complete care of us, then our faith ignites our giving. God has saved us. God has blessed us with more than enough and now we are actively looking to bless others. Now that we are part of the kingdom, we want to participate. We are overjoyed when we <u>get to</u> bless our brothers and sisters, and have a part in spreading the Gospel.

We pray the Lord bless you, today.

A Testimony....

One spring we needed a new push mower to mow inside the fence at our home on the farm. So, I headed off to the store and bought one. The previous one we had was self-propelled but we didn't think it was helpful in such a small area. And we had a riding mower and brush hog for the larger areas.

Within about a week I had to go and clear out my mother-in-law's garage because she had moved to be near us. Any guesses as to one of the things in her garage? Yep, a self-propelled lawnmower. She had moved into an apartment complex and didn't need it (and couldn't even store this mower).

I really was quite disturbed that God had not told me not to buy the new mower. I understand when I miss the leading of God, but how did God not see this coming. Well, at church I found out. A friend was telling me about how his lawnmower had run out of oil and was now a paperweight. He said that he was going to go get a new one the next day. He didn't have the money to replace it with a self-propelled model (which his old one was) so he was just going to get a regular push mower. Then it hit me, God didn't miss sending me the message (I know, I know... God never misses anything, ever). So, I conferred with my mother-in-law and she was able to bless him with her self-propelled mower. I told him the whole story about me wondering why God had not told me not to buy a new mower. Now I knew why, and now he could see God arranging to cover his loss even before it had happened.

(Bonus testimony - As I was paying for the new push mower, my son went outside to load the mower in our van. I gave him the keys, which he used to raise the back hatch. He set the keys down on the van floor, so he could have both hands to load the mower. But he forgot to pick them back up, so when he closed the hatch, we were locked out of the van. He came back in the store and told me what happened. Just then the Lord reminded me about the passenger door. When we had arrived, my mother-in-law had not shut her door very well. I noticed it but I knew the Lord didn't want me to correct it (I thought at the time it was to not embarrass her). So, we went out and checked. Sure enough, it was locked but had a gap. We bought some wire, slid it through the gap, and triggered the unlock button within a few minutes. It was great to be able to show my son, the protection, plans, and provision God had made to cover his mistake.)

Testify...

Pray...

Prophesy...

For the Lord your God has blessed you in all the work of your hands.

Deuteronomy 2:7a (HCSB)

Week #8

Good Morning, today we will be reading Matthew 13:44-46 (NLT).

⁴⁴ "The Kingdom of Heaven is like a treasure that a man discovered hidden in a field. In his excitement, he hid it again and sold everything he owned to get enough money to buy the field.
⁴⁵ "Again, the Kingdom of Heaven is like a merchant on the lookout for choice pearls. ⁴⁶ When he discovered a pearl of great value, he sold everything he owned and bought it!

The kingdom costs us everything. There is no getting around this. It costs you everything.

And Matthew 13:44-46 (NIV)
⁴⁴ "The kingdom of heaven is like treasure hidden in a field. When a man found it, he hid it again, and then in his joy went and sold all he had and bought that field.
⁴⁵ "Again, the kingdom of heaven is like a merchant looking for fine pearls. ⁴⁶ When he found one of great value, he went away and sold everything he had and bought it.

And finally, Matthew 13:44-46 (HCSB)
⁴⁴ "The kingdom of heaven is like treasure, buried in a field, that a man found and reburied. Then in his joy he goes and sells everything he has and buys that field.
⁴⁵ "Again, the kingdom of heaven is like a merchant in search of fine pearls. ⁴⁶ When he found one priceless pearl, he went and sold everything he had, and bought it.

Yes, it costs everything. But it is so beyond worth it. Do you see the excitement and the joy over that treasure? We had that excitement at salvation. We ran to Jesus, and gave him our wrecked lives. We gave him all that we were, and that certainly was not much, and we got everything. We got life, peace, joy, we got the Kingdom. Now how can we go back? The kingdom still costs me everything; today, and tomorrow. I have nothing of my own, it all belongs to Jesus. If He asks for the car, it is His. If He asks for the house, it is His. And it is always my excitement and my joy to give anything and everything for the Kingdom. Because I got the treasure, I got the pearl that was priceless. There is no way I could ever have enough to buy that treasure, but I found it hidden in Christ. This was not and is not drudgery. This is joy. This is about as close to stealing as you can get. I gave Him my rags and got a pure spotless garment. I gave Him my never having enough, for a cup that always overruns.

We pray the Lord bless you, today.

A Testimony....

When I was in my mid-twenties I went through a divorce, it not only left me emotionally devastated but in a really tough place financially. Then error after error, the financial stuff kept getting worse. My life was in ruins (literally and figuratively). I just wanted to leave, so I asked God if I could move to Tulsa, Oklahoma. Tulsa was where many of my great heroes in the faith were. God said, "Ok, but be ready at 30." I was happy to be able to 'get out of town,' but what was going to happen at 30? Tulsa was great for me in many ways spiritually, but financially things continued to worsen. So, after about 9 months, I moved back.

I had a new truck that I was making payments on. I bought an older house when I moved back that I had mortgage payments to make. And I had huge credit card debt (and I do mean huge). All through these moves and purchases, I could hear His words "be ready at 30." I knew "my life" was over at that 30 mark. I knew it could not and would not be about me after that. I really thought that God was going to send me off to somewhere in deepest Africa.

How could I possibly go with all this debt and promised repayments hanging over my head? I prayed and trusted God to bless me. I also didn't turn the heat on until I was freezing, nor did I turn the A/C on till I was sweating. I worked all the overtime that I was allowed. These 'efforts' were my part, but the numbers just didn't add up. Thank God, that His blessing supersedes numbers. God did bless me, exceeding and abundantly, and before I was 30 all my debts were paid. House, paid. Truck, paid. Credit cards, paid in full.

I had remarried in March of 2002, then in little over a year later in March of 2003, my daughter was born. My wife had six weeks of maternity leave, and then she had to go back to work. So two weeks before my 30th birthday, I quit my job. She went back to work, and I stayed home with my daughter. "My life" was over and my real life had begun. Because I heard my Father, and trusted in Him; I could now give up my life for my family. God's abundant blessings had delivered me from my mess and allowed me to become a blessing.

Testify...

Pray...

Prophesy...

He has watched over your journey through this immense wilderness. The LORD your God has been with you this past 40 years, and you have lacked nothing.'

Deuteronomy 2:7b (HCSB)

Week #9

Good Morning, today we will be reading **Psalms 34:8-10** (NLT)

> *⁸ Taste and see that the Lord is good.*
> *Oh, the joys of those who take refuge in Him!*
> *⁹ Fear the Lord, you His godly people,*
> *for those who fear Him will have all they need.*
> *¹⁰ Even strong young lions sometimes go hungry,*
> *but those who trust in the Lord will lack no good thing.*

And again **Psalms 34:8-10** (HCSB)

> *⁸ Taste and see that the Lord is good.*
> *How happy is the man who takes refuge in Him!*
> *⁹ You who are His holy ones, fear Yahweh,*
> *for those who fear Him lack nothing.*
> *¹⁰ Young lions lack food and go hungry,*
> *but those who seek the Lord*
> *will not lack any good thing*

And finally **Psalms 34:8-10** (NASB)

> *⁸ O taste and see that the Lord is good;*
> *How blessed is the man who takes refuge in Him!*
> *⁹ O fear the Lord, you His saints;*
> *For to those who fear Him there is no want.*
> *¹⁰ The young lions do lack and suffer hunger;*
> *But they who seek the Lord shall not be in want of any*
> *good thing.*

We must consider His Word and we must meditate on His nature, which is found in His Word. We cannot have real, true Faith in Him without knowing Him. Pressure will come, but if you know Him, you will stand in your faith. When everything looks bad and every logical thought says it will only get worse; Stand. Know your Father, take refuge in Him. You will see He is good. You will not suffer lack, you will have all you need, and you will abound in good things. You will be the blessed of the LORD.

We pray the Lord bless you, today.

A Testimony....

While our family was over in Japan, I began planning and searching for our forever home. I had always wanted about 10 acres with a cabin and a pond. Then I began to dream a little bigger. How about 40 acres, with an orchard? So, I scaled up the dream and even put pencil to paper. By the time I had planned out the 40 acres and did all the research on orchard production, it became very apparent that 40 acres was way too much. We would be overrun with fruit. So, I scaled back the dream to the original 10 acres.

Over the course of several years, I searched and searched. I wanted Colorado, but God pulled me to the east. So, I decided on west Texas, but again God pulled me east. Now, I am from western Oklahoma, so I like open spaces. I really didn't enjoy eastern Oklahoma that much. With all the trees and hills, it almost makes me claustrophobic. I just love to be able to see across an open field. I resisted and resisted, but I knew where I was supposed to go look.

I began to search for properties in eastern Oklahoma. I found one I liked (A) but it was already under contract. So, I found choices B and C. One day my wife peers over my shoulder, sees property A and says "That's home." Instantly, I wanted to correct her (she should have said, "that looks like home"). I didn't correct her, but I did explain it was not available because it was under contract.

Months and months went by and it stayed listed as under contract. I tried to call the realtor, but they never returned my calls. We now lived in North Dakota, but we were traveling back to Oklahoma to see our family. I had planned a trip to go over to eastern Oklahoma and see properties B and C. The property A (the dream) was right in on the way so, I decided to drive by and see it. Well, both B and C were just not right for us. But the dream property, albeit standing at the fence line, looked perfect. A few days later we were back in North Dakota and I set to renew my search. But now the dream property was up for sale by another realtor. I called immediately. My wife and I discussed it that night, and we made an offer the next day.

We bought the property, the 80 acres property. Yep, I wanted 10 and thought 40 was too much, so God gave me 80. He is an "exceedingly abundantly above" kind of Father. It is relatively flat and cleared, and it is "Home". We only actively use about 10 acres of the land, and God has shown us that the other 70 acres are to be used to bless our brothers and sisters in the Lord. We were and are blessed with 'too much', and with all that 'too much' we will bless...

Testify...

Pray...

Prophesy...

Therefore
I will look
to the LORD;
I will wait
for the God of
my salvation;
My God
will hear me.

Micah 7:7 (NKJV)

Week #10

Good Morning, today we will be reading 1 Kings 3:5-14 (NLT).

⁵ That night the Lord appeared to Solomon in a dream, and God said, "What do you want? Ask, and I will give it to you!"

⁶ Solomon replied, "You showed great and faithful love to your servant my father, David, because he was honest and true and faithful to you. And you have continued to show this great and faithful love to him today by giving him a son to sit on his throne.

⁷ "Now, O Lord my God, you have made me king instead of my father, David, but I am like a little child who doesn't know his way around. ⁸ And here I am in the midst of your own chosen people, a nation so great and numerous they cannot be counted! ⁹ Give me an understanding heart so that I can govern your people well and know the difference between right and wrong. For who by himself is able to govern this great people of yours?"

¹⁰ The Lord was pleased that Solomon had asked for wisdom. ¹¹ So God replied, "Because you have asked for wisdom in governing my people with justice and have not asked for a long life or wealth or the death of your enemies— ¹² I will give you what you asked for! I will give you a wise and understanding heart such as no one else has had or ever will have! ¹³ And I will also give you what you did not ask for—riches and fame! No other king in all the world will be compared to you for the rest of your life! ¹⁴ And if you follow me and obey my decrees and my commands as your father, David, did, I will give you a long life."

It is a heart issue. Hear what Solomon really asked for, "Give me an **understanding heart so that I can govern your people well.**" And hear God reply, "Because you have asked for **wisdom in governing my people.**" If we are only focused on ourselves, then money can and will hurt us. But if we love God and thereby love the people; money is simply a tool by which we can bless our brothers and sisters and further the Kingdom. Then we can have all we can handle. Then we can have abundance and overflow. If our heart isn't right money will always be a problem. But when our heart is right, when Love changes us from selfish to selfless, wealth is never a stumbling block.

We pray the Lord bless you, today.

A Testimony....

Each year my family and I go to a week-long church convention. One year I had given the kids some spending money ($100 each) to use however they wished over that week. Nearing the end of that week they had not spent hardly any money. So, I had a little talk with them about deciding what they wanted to do with their money. We were planning to go to a nearby mall between services, so they could spend it there. I also encouraged them to participate in the convention by giving some of their money in the offering. This way they were not just receiving great teaching but they could, through giving, have a part in sending out the teaching. I explained they had a chance to be a part of leading worship, teaching the bible, praying for the sick, and leading their peers to know Jesus, simply by giving.

A day went by and the kids made no request to access their funds. Two days before the convention was over, I again broached the subject. I tried to make it clear that it was their decision but time was running out if they did want to give. They said they had been thinking about what to do with their money, and they had decided.

As their dad, I was honestly hoping they would simply participate in giving. I was just looking for them to understand the concept. So a few dollars would have been great, and a substantial gift of $20 would have been Good.

My son spoke first and said he wanted to give all his remaining money away in the offering. I just about hit the floor. Then my daughter spoke, she wanted to break her money into thirds. Ok, let's pause time here for a moment. She is the older child and if she had gone first giving a third of her money would have made me want to do a cartwheel, but her younger brother wanted to give it all. Ok, restart time. She then said she wanted to give a third to her brother, a third to her parents (to help us pay for the trip), and give a third in the offering. Ok, I can't really describe the joy that I experienced in that moment. But I can tell you that they could have asked me for anything at the moment. Any request, reasonable or unreasonable, would have been granted in that moment. New clothes, new toys, new bike, or a new car; anything and everything was on the table. Because I could see their hearts were right, I could see they loved people and the Kingdom more than themselves. Now that the concern of "spoiling" them is removed, I could be lavish and go beyond their needs well over into their wants. They understood that the money could have provided things and experiences for them, but they chose to consider others first. That is all that is necessary to loose the dad to bless.

That is all that is necessary to loose the Father to bless.

Testify...

Pray...

Prophesy...

But you, Timothy, are a man of God; so run from all these evil things. Pursue righteousness and a godly life, along with faith, love, perseverance, and gentleness.

1 Timothy 6:11 (NLT)

Week #11

Good Morning, today we will be reading Psalms 112 (NKJV).

¹Praise the Lord! Blessed is the man who fears the Lord, who delights greatly in His commandments. ²His descendants will be mighty on earth; The generation of the upright will be blessed. ³Wealth and riches will be in his house, And his righteousness endures forever. ⁴Unto the upright there arises light in the darkness; He is gracious, and full of compassion, and righteous. ⁵A good man deals graciously and lends; He will guide his affairs with discretion. ⁶Surely he will never be shaken; The righteous will be in everlasting remembrance. ⁷He will not be afraid of evil tidings; His heart is steadfast, trusting in the Lord. ⁸His heart is established; He will not be afraid, Until he sees his desire upon his enemies. ⁹He has dispersed abroad, He has given to the poor; His righteousness endures forever; His horn will be exalted with honor. ¹⁰The wicked will see it and be grieved; He will gnash his teeth and melt away; The desire of the wicked shall perish.

And Psalms 112 (NLT)

¹Praise the Lord! How joyful are those who fear the Lord and delight in obeying his commands. ²Their children will be successful everywhere; an entire generation of godly people will be blessed. ³They themselves will be wealthy, and their good deeds will last forever. ⁴Light shines in the darkness for the godly. They are generous, compassionate, and righteous. ⁵Good comes to those who lend money generously and conduct their business fairly. ⁶Such people will not be overcome by evil. Those who are righteous will be long remembered. ⁷They do not fear bad news; they confidently trust the Lord to care for them. ⁸They are confident and fearless and can face their foes triumphantly. ⁹They share freely and give generously to those in need. Their good deeds will be remembered forever. They will have influence and honor. ¹⁰The wicked will see this and be infuriated. They will grind their teeth in anger; they will slink away, their hopes thwarted.

Wealth; yes. Trusting in the Lord; yes. Sharing freely and giving generously; yes, and yes. Exalted, righteous, and remembered; yes, yes, and yes. Having influence and honor; yes, and yes. Infuriating our enemy; oh, yes. Let us walk with our Father, abide in Him, and know His blessings.

We pray the Lord bless you, today.

A Testimony....

Years ago, the church we attended began to see an influx of refugees who had just come into the US. Most of them were all living in an area quite far from our church. They didn't have vehicles or driver's licenses yet. So as a church, we began to send people out to bring them to services. My family wanted to participate but we only had two small cars. We were happy to go get three at a time but we wanted to do more.

We had bought the farm so; we were looking to buy a pickup. We decided, however, in order to help get more people to church, that we would buy a minivan. This way we could bring twice as many people to church.

I researched and researched and found two good candidates for my family to consider. We headed out one day to decide on which one to purchase. We liked both and went to go get lunch to discuss it as a family. One had a bigger engine, foldable seats, and more features; and the other one was less expensive. We talked it over and decided we would never need the extra features. So, we headed out to buy the less expensive van. We paid for it and then headed home. I only drove a couple of blocks and I knew something wasn't right. It was horribly out of alignment. But I knew I could get that fixed, so I continued on my way home. Then a couple of miles later, I heard God say, "No." Now, this was not that still calm voice. This was firm and emphatic. I pulled over and wanted to argue, but that "No" was still ringing in my spirit. So, I headed back to the dealership and returned the vehicle. We then went to the other dealer to buy the other van. We got there just in time as they were about to close for a holiday weekend. We bought the van and headed home, this time with the blessing of God.

It struck me that in all my research and in all our discussions we never asked for God to lead us and show us the way. Many months later as we were driving on an interstate off-ramp, God showed me why He was so forceful. Right there, in that major city, in that maze of on and off-ramps some 40 feet off the ground, that other van would have had a problem. God showed me that accident and none of my family would have survived. On our way to a church convention, we would have gone home to heaven way too soon. But God...

The van we did buy turned out to be a heroic vehicle. It carried many, many refugees to church. I made many 1,000-mile trips to our farm in that van. It hauled cargo, towed trailers, and later it even towed a one-ton flatbed truck. It was a blessing to us, and hands down the best vehicle we have ever owned.

We need God to be involved in our life, all aspects of our life. Financial decisions including purchases both large and small should be discussed with our Good Father. He always knows what is best for us, ***always***.

Testify...

Pray...

Prophesy...

Fight the good fight for the true faith. Hold tightly to the eternal life to which God has called you, which you have declared so well before many witnesses.

1 Timothy 6:12 (NLT)

Week #12

Good Morning, today we will be reading **Psalms 52:7** (NASB).

> **"BEHOLD, THE MAN WHO WOULD NOT MAKE GOD HIS REFUGE,**
> **BUT TRUSTED IN THE ABUNDANCE OF HIS RICHES**
> **AND WAS STRONG IN HIS EVIL DESIRE."**

And **Psalm 52:7** (NLT)

> **"LOOK WHAT HAPPENS TO MIGHTY WARRIORS**
> **WHO DO NOT TRUST IN GOD.**
> **THEY TRUST THEIR WEALTH INSTEAD**
> **AND GROW MORE AND MORE BOLD IN THEIR WICKEDNESS."**

And finally, **Psalm 52:7** (NKJV)

> **"HERE IS THE MAN WHO DID NOT MAKE GOD HIS STRENGTH,**
> **BUT TRUSTED IN THE ABUNDANCE OF HIS RICHES,**
> **AND STRENGTHENED HIMSELF IN HIS WICKEDNESS."**

Does this mean that an abundance of riches (wealth) is to be fiercely avoided? No, this is a **trust** issue. Trusting in wealth is very dangerous. When you insist "I got this", you are preventing God from helping in your life. Always put your trust in God. God is the only thing that will never fail. There is a limit to your wealth, there is a limit to your logic and reason, there is a limit to your physical abilities, but there is no limit to your Father. No matter how smart we are, how strong we get, or how financially secure we appear to be; always stay close to Papa. Always run to him, always hold your faith, that He loves you and He provides for you.

Let us look at the next verse. **Psalm 52:8** (NKJV)

> **⁸ BUT I AM LIKE A GREEN OLIVE TREE IN THE HOUSE OF GOD;**
> **I TRUST IN THE MERCY OF GOD FOREVER AND EVER.**

You can flourish; you can be a fruitful tree. You can have abundance, but do not trust in that abundance. When your trust is firmly in Him, you will be able to handle the blessings of God. Then your focus will always be on your Father, and the wealth will be simply a means to bless others.

We pray the Lord bless you, today.

A Testimony....

One summer I was searching and searching for another tractor for our farm. The first one we bought was not running. We had simply pushed that small tractor too hard over the years. I was hardly ever at the farm so it wasn't a pressing matter for me. But my step-dad was living there and he needed a tractor. With a working tractor he could tackle a lot of projects, but without it there just wasn't a lot for him to do. I knew he wanted to be active, so I began looking high and low for one. I checked online postings. I went to auctions. I tracked online auctions in half a dozen states. But nothing ever worked out. I was going to need a lot of versatility out of this tractor. And I simply didn't have enough money to purchase something that could handle our farm's needs.

Months had gone by and still, I had not found a tractor. One day while driving down to the farm the Lord spoke to me. He said, "Challenge Me." Of course, my religion wanted to argue with Him, but I know from experience who wins those debates.

"...AND TRY ME NOW IN THIS..." Malachi 3:10 (NKJV)

"WHERE IS THE LORD GOD OF ELIJAH?" 2 Kings 2:14 (NKJV)

So, I turned from my abilities and my money and I challenged God. It really is His farm anyway (I just work for Him). And it is His son that I am trying help. So, ok God; what can *You* do?

Well, He can do exceedingly abundantly above. Within ten days a pipeline company redirected their route and contracted with me to bring their pipeline down the edge of my property. It was deep enough to never affect me, and I got some of the wild areas of my property cleaned up and cleared. I received nearly half of my total yearly income as compensation. To date, I have bought four tractors with that money and still have funds remaining.

God is God, and He is a Good Father. I just needed to turn to Him, and trust in Him. He can do mighty things on our behalf, but we have to open that door for Him. Faith, not works, opens that door.

Testify...

_____
_____
_____
_____
_____
_____
_____

Pray...

_____
_____
_____
_____
_____
_____
_____

Prophesy...

_____
_____
_____
_____
_____

And he Believed in the LORD, and He accounted it to him for righteousness.

Genesis 15:6 (NKJV)

Week #13

Good Morning, today we will be reading **1 Chronicles 13:11-14** (NLT).

¹¹ David was angry because the Lord's anger had burst out against Uzzah. He named that place Perez-uzzah (which means "to burst out against Uzzah"), as it is still called today.

¹² David was now afraid of God, and he asked, "How can I ever bring the Ark of God back into my care?" ¹³ So David did not move the Ark into the City of David. Instead, he took it to the house of Obed-edom of Gath. ¹⁴ The Ark of God remained there in Obed-edom's house for three months, and the Lord blessed the household of Obed-edom and everything he owned.

David was hurt, upset, afraid, and mad at God. But it was the blessings of God on Obed-edom that softened his heart and got his attention. He expected tragedy to follow the ark. He expected the fierceness of God. But day after day He saw the blessing of God on Obed-edom and on "everything he owned". This led David to talk to God about what happened to Uzzah, and to search the scriptures. He found the answer as we see in **1 Chronicles 15:13, 15** (NLT).

¹³ Because you Levites did not carry the Ark the first time, the anger of the Lord our God burst out against us. We failed to ask God how to move it properly.

¹⁵ Then the Levites carried the Ark of God on their shoulders with its carrying poles, just as the Lord had instructed Moses.

Let us always have faith that the blessings of the Lord in all areas of our life will provoke our brothers and sisters, and even the lost of this world, to seek out the true heart of God. Let the Goodness of the Lord turn the hearts of the world to chase after Him. (**Romans 2:4**)

We pray the Lord bless you, today.

A Testimony....

The Lord led me to fund a young man in a business endeavor. We talked about it and I gave the young man some advice and told him I would put up $3,000 to help him get started. But then I kept giving more advice and even got hands-on in the project. Things did not go as planned and we had a mess. This business endeavor was now going to lose money, not make it. The thing God had planned to be a blessing for the young man was now quite the opposite.

The Lord let me recognize my error and I let go of 'my knowledge, skill, and abilities.' I refocused on those things I was assigned by the Father to do and waited for Him to take the lead in that business endeavor. As we then let God lead, things got much better. The young man was blessed, and so was I. We were even able to help another brother step out in faith. He was able to see the hand of God bring real blessings speedily to him in an answer to a need.

The Father simply could not bless the work of my hand when I insisted on doing it on my own. Thanks be to God, that He is gracious and merciful. He does not hold grudges or any ill will toward us. He is faithful and just to forgive.

IF WE CONFESS OUR SINS, HE IS FAITHFUL AND JUST TO FORGIVE US OUR SINS AND TO CLEANSE US FROM ALL UNRIGHTEOUSNESS.
1 John 1:9 (NKJV)

When we turn (repent) from our own works and run to Papa, He is right there ready to help. He always knows just how to fix it all, and incredibly, He can make something wonderful out of our mess.

We need to walk closely with our Father and never let go of His hand. Money and knowledge can sometimes deceive us into thinking that we can handle what only God is meant to handle. He is the Father; we are the children. He is the one with the master plan and He is the one that makes all things work together for the good.

(Romans 8:28)

Testify...

_____
_____
_____
_____
_____
_____
_____

Pray...

_____
_____
_____
_____
_____
_____
_____

Prophesy...

_____
_____
_____
_____
_____

As for God, His way is perfect; The word of the LORD is proven; He is a shield to all who trust in Him.

Psalm 18:30 (NKJV)

Week #14

Good Morning, today we will be reading 2 Samuel 9:1-13 (NASB).

¹ Then David said, "Is there yet anyone left of the house of Saul, that I may show him kindness for Jonathan's sake?" ² Now there was a servant of the house of Saul whose name was Ziba, and they called him to David; and the king said to him, "Are you Ziba?" And he said, "I am your servant." ³ The king said, "Is there not yet anyone of the house of Saul to whom I may show the kindness of God?" And Ziba said to the king, "There is still a son of Jonathan who is crippled in both feet." ⁴ So the king said to him, "Where is he?" And Ziba said to the king, "Behold, he is in the house of Machir the son of Ammiel in Lo-debar." ⁵ Then King David sent and brought him from the house of Machir the son of Ammiel, from Lo-debar. ⁶ Mephibosheth, the son of Jonathan the son of Saul, came to David and fell on his face and prostrated himself. And David said, "Mephibosheth." And he said, "Here is your servant!" ⁷ David said to him, "Do not fear, for I will surely show kindness to you for the sake of your father Jonathan, and will restore to you all the land of your grandfather Saul; and you shall eat at my table regularly." ⁸ Again he prostrated himself and said, "What is your servant, that you should regard a dead dog like me?"

⁹ Then the king called Saul's servant Ziba and said to him, "All that belonged to Saul and to all his house I have given to your master's grandson. ¹⁰ You and your sons and your servants shall cultivate the land for him, and you shall bring in the produce so that your master's grandson may have food; nevertheless Mephibosheth your master's grandson shall eat at my table regularly." Now Ziba had fifteen sons and twenty servants. ¹¹ Then Ziba said to the king, "According to all that my lord the king commands his servant so your servant will do." So Mephibosheth ate at David's table as one of the king's sons. ¹² Mephibosheth had a young son whose name was Mica. And all who lived in the house of Ziba were servants to Mephibosheth. ¹³ So Mephibosheth lived in Jerusalem, for he ate at the king's table regularly. Now he was lame in both feet.

Who are we that God would bless us? We have no abilities and we come from a broken lineage. But it is not because of us that we are blessed. It is for the sake of our Lord Jesus, that the Father shows us all these blessings. Our favor is because of Him. Our position is because of Him. Our wealth is because of Him. We need to allow the blessings of God into our life, even though we do not deserve them. Let our most gracious Father restore us, establish us, and lead us to abundance.

We pray the Lord bless you, today.

A Testimony....

Many years ago, my niece, who was just starting out in the world, began to ask her grandmother (my mother) financial questions. My mother told her that I was very good with money and that she should ask me her questions. My heart swelled when I heard that, and so did my head. But then I began to look back at my financial decisions.

Stock market investments.
The first company I bought stock in went completely bankrupt and I lost everything. Then years later, I tried day-trading. I lost thousands.

Business.
I opened up a small business, but it did very nearly nothing. I closed it down within a year, and I still have inventory in storage.

Vehicles.
Once I had to decide between two minivans. Keep one and sell one. Well, the one I kept; its motor was destroyed within just a few months.

And the list of financial failures that involves trying to take the cheapest way possible, is a very long list indeed. It is amazing how much more expensive the 'cheapest' way turns out to be.

As I reflected on these things, I really began to wonder how in the world did our family ever achieve even a modicum of financial success? I knew it was not my wisdom, my knowledge, my skill, or my ability. It was in fact in spite of all these things. It was my Father's blessing.

Listening to the Father, letting Him take the lead, that is when and where all my family's blessings have always been. And that is where the blessing and the blessings will forever abide. Our skills, abilities, knowledge, and wisdom can be good and useful things, but they can never be allowed to lead. Using those God-given abilities, under His direction, will always turn out for the good.

I did endeavor to answer my niece's practical financial questions, but even more, I tried to pass on to her that walking with God will always be your key to success.

Devoted Money

Testify...

Pray...

Prophesy...

A servant of the Lord must not quarrel but must be kind to everyone, be able to teach, and be patient with difficult people. Gently instruct those who oppose the truth. Perhaps God will change those people's hearts, and they will learn the truth.

2 Timothy 2:24-25 (NLT)

Week #15

Good Morning, today we will be reading **1 Chronicles 4:9-10** (NKJV).

⁹ Now Jabez was more honorable than his brothers, and his mother called his name Jabez, saying, "Because I bore him in pain." ¹⁰ And Jabez called on the God of Israel saying, "Oh, that You would bless me indeed, and enlarge my territory, that Your hand would be with me, and that You would keep me from evil, that I may not cause pain!" So God granted him what he requested.

And **1 Chronicles 4:9-10** (HCSB)

⁹ Jabez was more honorable than his brothers. His mother named him Jabez and said, "I gave birth to him in pain." ¹⁰ Jabez called out to the God of Israel: "If only You would bless me, extend my border, let Your hand be with me, and keep me from harm, so that I will not cause any pain." And God granted his request.

Jabez always had that name just hanging on him like a lead anchor. All his life he is hearing that he brings pain, sorrow, and grief when he hears that name. He so wants to be out from under that name. He wants to never bring pain or cause grief. He wants to bless. He wants to bring joy. Now this is a heart's cry that our Father loves to hear. This is a request that our Father is most happy to grant. Lord, give us a heart to cry out for your blessing so that we can be a blessing. More than enough, and a cup that overflows; so that we can be a blessing. So that we can bring joy, undue those heavy burdens, and bring relief from all that pain and grief. When our heart is right, when it is set on being a help to others, then we can walk in more blessings and abundance than we ever thought possible.

We pray the Lord bless you, today.

A Testimony....

A minister that I dearly love was at one time building a church in the Baltic states. He sent out a letter describing the proposed building and the cost. He had it broken down into cost per square foot. It was about $20/\text{ft}^2$. I was just out on my own and really did not have much of anything, but I love this minister and eagerly wanted to participate. The first month I did all I could, I sent him $20 and I help build one square foot. I had determined that I would send him $20 each month until it was done. But the next month things were tight, and so I held back my gift. The following month again I just couldn't let the money go. But... I said the next month I would double up and send $40. When I opened up that next letter from him, the building had been paid in full. I was happy for him and his ministry, but I was crushed by what I had done.

I had put off a kingdom project and missed my chance to be more involved. Now, if $20 was all I had or all I had purposed in my heart to give, then great. But that was not all I had and it was not all I purposed in my heart to give. That church has been built and functioning for well over 20 years. I have had my one square foot all that time, in every service, in every event, and in every good thing that has happened there. But to this day I long to have the three square feet that I should have had.

Now, God is of course loving, kind, gracious, and forgiving, but I have never forgotten the lesson I learned.

Be quick to obey

Participating in the Kingdom is a valuable thing, it is an honorable thing, and it is a precious thing. It should never be laborious and it should never be looked upon as a drudgery.

His Kingdom will grow, move, and increase. The question is do we really want to be a part of it. Or do we want to *slow-walk it*, and hope someone else takes over our part?

This lesson has been invaluable to me over the decades. But I do wish I would have listened to the Father and let Him teach me, instead of learning the lesson through experience.

Testify...

Pray...

Prophesy...

He made Him who knew no sin to be sin on our behalf, so that we might become the righteousness of God in Him.

2 Corinthians 5:21 (NASB)

Week #16

Good Morning, today we will be reading **Proverbs 11:24** (NASB).

> *²⁴ There is one who scatters, and yet increases all the more,*
> *And there is one who withholds what is justly due, and yet it results only in want.*

And **Proverbs 11:24** (NKJV)

> *²⁴ There is one who scatters, yet increases more;*
> *And there is one who withholds more than is right,*
> *But it leads to poverty.*

And again **Proverbs 11:24** (HCSB)

> *²⁴ One person gives freely,*
> *yet gains more;*
> *another withholds what is right,*
> *only to become poor.*

And finally, **Proverbs 11:24** (NLT)

> *²⁴ Give freely and become more wealthy;*
> *be stingy and lose everything.*

Our Father loves to bless us with all good things, but we are not designed to hold all of those good things for ourselves. We are created to be rivers. We are made to receive great blessings from our Father and then used them to bless our brothers and sisters. We cannot let ourselves become like a lake or a reservoir, where we hold all those blessings for ourselves. We should allow God to pour blessings in and we must be about finding ways to pour out those blessings. The greatness of His Kingdom is that the river will always stay full. No matter how much or how fast you pour out with your giving, the river stays full.

> *God will always exceed what you pour out,*
> *with what He pours in.*

We pray the Lord bless you, today.

A Testimony....

One year at a church convention I went over to their bookstore area. I picked up a few things and headed to the checkout counters. A lady right next to me was having some difficulty. She did not have her credit card with her and she was just short of having enough cash. I knew what the Lord wanted me to do, so I paid for her purchase. She was buying a very good book, and it was only about $20.

Of course, she said I didn't have to do that. She offered to give me what cash she had and even offered to repay me in full. I just sincerely asked if I could just bless her and buy her the book. She agreed and said, "Thank you." I, of course, responded with the obligatory, "You're welcome."

But there was something different about those phrases, in that moment. At that moment, those societal norms meant something more. These were heartfelt exchanges between family. I had never met her before and have not seen her since. I do not know her name or where on this planet she resides. But what I do know is she's my sister.

She is my sister and I am her brother. It was her brother helping her that day, not a stranger. This simple act of being a blessing revealed what is not apparent in this world. Using money, to be a blessing, revealed family. She knew I was her brother, and I knew that was my sister.

What a great comfort to know that we have a multitude of family around us most every day. What a great blessing to know that we are not out there on our own.

Remember Elijah, **1 Kings 19:14** (NKJV) ...*I ALONE AM LEFT*... But that feeling simply wasn't true, **I Kings 19:18** (NKJV) *YET I HAVE RESERVED SEVEN THOUSAND IN ISRAEL, ALL WHOSE KNEES HAVE NOT BOWED TO BAAL, AND EVERY MOUTH THAT HAS NOT KISSED HIM."*

Giving generously and endeavoring to be a blessing reveals our heart and our true nature. The heart of love and nature of selflessness, reveals that we are our Father's children. We can show who we are and who's we are with these simple acts of giving.

That day, I saw the world in a new light, abounding with my brothers and sisters. They are the sons and daughters of God, and they are ready, willing, and well able to help.

Thank you, Papa, we sure love this Kingdom.

Testify...

Pray...

Prophesy...

By this all men will know that you are My disciples, if you have love for one another."

John 13:35 (NASB)

Week #17

Good Morning, today we will be reading **1 Chronicles 29:9** (NASB).

This is when King David and the leaders of the people brought offerings for the building of the temple.

Then the people rejoiced because they had offered so willingly, for they made their offering to the Lord with a whole heart, and King David also rejoiced greatly.

And **1 Chronicles 29:9** (NKJV)

Then the people rejoiced, for they had offered willingly, because with a loyal heart they had offered willingly to the Lord; and King David also rejoiced greatly.

And again **1 Chronicles 29:9** (HCSB)

Then the people rejoiced because of their leaders' willingness to give, for they had given to the Lord with a whole heart. King David also rejoiced greatly.

And finally, **1 Chronicles 29:9** (NLT)

The people rejoiced over the offerings, for they had given freely and wholeheartedly to the Lord, and King David was filled with joy.

Rejoicing over giving. Rejoicing over a freely given gift that is given wholeheartedly. Rejoicing because your leaders and king have given to the Lord. That wholehearted free gift, shows faith and trust in God. Faith and trust in God opens the door for Him to move. King David is turning his kingdom to his son. The offerings given by the leaders show their heart toward God. This shows David the kingdom is set for the right path. This filled King David with joy and he rejoiced greatly.

We pray the Lord bless you, today.

A Testimony....

I have mentioned in some of the previous testimonies, how wonderfully and miraculously God had changed my heart concerning money and giving. My original nature was to live in fear of lack. That fear drives people to hold onto whatever they have. Whether they have a little or even if they have plenty, that fear will never let them relax. It always envisions the worst of circumstances are just around the corner. So, there is never any real rest and there can never be any liberality, peace, or joy in giving. Because whenever and whatever I may force myself to give that fear of lack is always screaming "what if."

But great is our God, and His deliverance brings freedom. Love sustains trust, and trust allows for peace. God loves us and He will never fail us. We can trust Him and we can rest in Him.

One Sunday morning I heard that the church's soundboard had stopped working. They had borrowed a small one from a musician just to get through Sunday morning service. Then they had to decide if they were going to repair or replace the board.

I could hardly sit through service. It was hard to concentrate on the message. I was so eager to get to the pastor. I rushed right to him immediately after service. I asked politely (but firmly) if I could please buy the new board. I was so hoping that no one had already volunteered. The board handled all the music and singing in praise and worship. That board handled all the sermons, all the announcements, calls to prayer, and words of encouragement and hope. Most everything was running through that board and I so badly wanted to be the one the provide it. I desired to provide that key piece in helping the church and the kingdom function.

But the whole time that I am eagerly awaiting service to finish, I was in awe of my own heart (the new one God had given me). I didn't have any idea what a soundboard would cost, I didn't care. I didn't know how it would affect *my* life or my family budget; I didn't care.

I wanted to bless that church. I wanted to help the kingdom. I was not concerned about me because I knew my Father is faithful. I can relax and rest in Him. I can be free to give excitedly, generously, and without fear, because *He has me.*

Testify...

_____
_____
_____
_____
_____
_____
_____

Pray...

_____
_____
_____
_____
_____
_____
_____

Prophesy...

_____
_____
_____
_____
_____

Therefore, we are ambassadors for Christ, as though God were making an appeal through us; we beg you on behalf of Christ, be reconciled to God.

2 Corinthians 5:20 (NASB)

Week #18

Good Morning, today we will be reading Psalm 11:1 (NKJV).

> **IN THE LORD I PUT MY TRUST;**
> **HOW CAN YOU SAY TO MY SOUL,**
> **"FLEE AS A BIRD TO YOUR MOUNTAIN"?**

And Psalm 11:1 (NASB)
> **IN THE LORD I TAKE REFUGE;**
> **HOW CAN YOU SAY TO MY SOUL, "FLEE AS A BIRD TO YOUR MOUNTAIN;**

And again Psalm 11:1 (NLT)
> **I TRUST IN THE LORD FOR PROTECTION.**
> **SO WHY DO YOU SAY TO ME,**
> **"FLY LIKE A BIRD TO THE MOUNTAINS FOR SAFETY!**

And finally, Psalm 11:1 (HCSB)
> **I HAVE TAKEN REFUGE IN THE LORD.**
> **HOW CAN YOU SAY TO ME,**
> **"ESCAPE TO THE MOUNTAIN LIKE A BIRD!**

We trust in the Lord. He is our good Father. We know Him. We know His kindness and His mercy. We know that He will not fail us. We trust in the Lord; we must learn to trust Him in all areas of our life including our finances. The world will scream, "Run to the mountain!" The world will panic, when things look bad. The world will run to their well thought out plans, when loss seems inevitable. But we run to the Lord. We trust Him when there is abundance and we trust Him when there is lack. Lord, our patient Father, help us to never let fear, worry, anxiety, stress over what *appears* to be; drive us to the mountain. We take our refuge in You.

> **OFFER SACRIFICES IN THE RIGHT SPIRIT, AND TRUST THE LORD.**
>
> Psalms 4:5 (NLT)

We pray the Lord bless you, today.

A Testimony....

One summer the air conditioning stop working at our farm. I tried to repair it, but that failed. So, we called a repairman. He ordered and installed new parts but even that did not fix the problem. It would now require a new unit. I had steeled myself for about a $500 repair bill, but now the replacement cost was $4,000.

I could feel that old nature try and reassert itself. My mind wanted to find a cheaper way. There was a cheaper way out; I could install window A/C's in the home for about a third that price. I even did that kind of work in college, so why not?

I knew what the right thing to do was. I knew what God wanted me to do. I did have the money to do the real repair, that old nature just didn't want to let go of that money. Our farm is not really *our* farm, it is my Father's. I just work for Him, managing *His* property you might say. Also, my money is not my money, it's His. I gave up everything at salvation (I died when I went under that water in baptism). I gave up *my* life, and received new life in Him. Dead men can't own anything, and they can't have financial accounts. Now, I am free of such things and can abide in His life, His blessing, and His abundance. And I am free to simply walk with my Father.

Our farm is also meant to be a place for visitors to rest and be refreshed in the Lord. So, if the farm isn't mine, I should differ to the owner on repairs. If the buildings are designed to help others then I should do what is right for them. We did as the Father instructed, we released that money and got the new A/C.

I still had to battle that old nature even after everything was done. My mind wanted to find a way to cut our budget and slash our spending until we could make up for the loss. But His Spirit strengthened my spirit and I was able to rest in Him.

Within a matter of just a couple of months, God also called us to give a vehicle away, and then loan out a significant (to us) amount of money. We had spent, given, and loaned over $20,000 in a couple of months, and that is very significant to my family.

But this is what we have been recreated in Him to be; to be a help and to be a blessing. Our lives are not about us anymore. We are living for Him, His Kingdom, and His people.

My family never suffered lack or distress. We did not have to cut back. We never had to miss out on any good thing. God is and always will be faithful, and we simply walk with and work for Him.

Testify...

Pray...

Prophesy...

20 Now may
the God of peace—
who brought up
from the dead
our Lord Jesus,
the great Shepherd
of the sheep,
and ratified
an eternal covenant
with his blood—
21 may he equip you with
all you need
for doing his will.

Hebrews 13:20-21a (NLT)

Week #19

Good Morning, today we will be reading Psalm 25:12-13 (NKJV).

> **¹² WHO IS THE MAN THAT FEARS THE LORD?**
> **HIM SHALL HE TEACH IN THE WAY HE CHOOSES.**
> **¹³ HE HIMSELF SHALL DWELL IN PROSPERITY,**
> **AND HIS DESCENDANTS SHALL INHERIT THE EARTH.**

And Psalm 25:12-13 (NASB)

> **¹² WHO IS THE MAN WHO FEARS THE LORD?**
> **HE WILL INSTRUCT HIM IN THE WAY HE SHOULD CHOOSE.**
> **¹³ HIS SOUL WILL ABIDE IN PROSPERITY,**
> **AND HIS DESCENDANTS WILL INHERIT THE LAND.**

And Psalm 25:12-13 (HCSB)

> **¹² WHO IS THE MAN WHO FEARS THE LORD?**
> **HE WILL SHOW HIM THE WAY HE SHOULD CHOOSE.**
> **¹³ HE WILL LIVE A GOOD LIFE,**
> **AND HIS DESCENDANTS WILL INHERIT THE LAND.**

And again Psalm 25:12-13 (NLT)

> **¹² WHO ARE THOSE WHO FEAR THE LORD?**
> **HE WILL SHOW THEM THE PATH THEY SHOULD CHOOSE.**
> **¹³ THEY WILL LIVE IN PROSPERITY,**
> **AND THEIR CHILDREN WILL INHERIT THE LAND.**

And finally, Psalm 25:12-13 (KJV)

> **¹² WHAT MAN IS HE THAT FEARETH THE LORD? HIM SHALL HE TEACH IN THE WAY THAT HE SHALL CHOOSE.**
> **¹³ HIS SOUL SHALL DWELL AT EASE; AND HIS SEED SHALL INHERIT THE EARTH.**

The word that is translated prosperity is the Hebrew word towb (tobe) and it is a very broad brush. It means good in every direction.

Here we see it translated as good life, prosperity, and at ease. Is it only talking about finances? Of course not. Is it talking about every area of your life except finances? Of course not. Respect and honor God, He will teach you the way to go. Respect and honor God so that when He does show you the path to walk, that you actually do walk that path. Then you will prosper in *all* areas of your life.

We pray the Lord bless you, today.

A Testimony....

Most of my walk I have attended very small churches, and they are an amazing place to grow in God and grow together in the body of Christ. I did for some time attend a "mega" church. I had loved hearing this pastor on the radio and when I had moved close enough to attend, I jumped at the chance.

One Sunday morning as service was ending, the pastor stopped and looked right at a lady in the audience. He asked if everything was alright? She shook her head yes but streams of tears began to flow down her face.

He called her to the front and she told her story. She had moved to this city with her small children to leave a dangerously bad situation. She had enough money to rent an apartment for one month, but that was all she had. She had no food, no beds, no dishes, no job, no nothing.

This church had a site where you could drop off your old furniture, appliances, etc. They would then give those things away to those in need. So, the pastor asked if there was furniture available. There was, so the lady now had furniture. Then another lady in the congregation stood up and said, "She has dishes." Several people popped up with many statements like, "She has clothes for the kids" etc... Then a gentleman at the back of the church stood up and asked the lady what her works experience/skills were? As she began to answer, he told her to come to his place of business on Monday. He told the pastor, "She has a job."

Now the woman was again in tears but for a whole other set of reasons. She had come to church (the body of Christ) with nothing. And in a few brief moments, the church had taken her from nothing to abundance. Then the church took up an offering! With the love of God moving through that place, I know that was no small offering.

This is one of the top three miracles I have ever seen in my life (in person). This was the church being what we are called to be. We did not say, we'll pray for you and sent her away empty (**James 2:14-17**). We acted like our Father and we had helped, encouraged, and blessed our sister in the Lord. That day I saw the church, be The Church. All of our doctrine, our beliefs, our faith, and our love moved us to action. We gave part of our life to make another whole. It has and always will be a great encouragement to me of what we (the Church) can and will be.

Testify...

_____
_____
_____
_____
_____
_____
_____

Pray...

_____
_____
_____
_____
_____
_____
_____

Prophesy...

_____
_____
_____
_____
_____

May he produce in you, through the power of Jesus Christ, every good thing that is pleasing to him. All glory to him forever and ever! Amen.

Hebrews 13:21b (NLT)

Week #20

Good Morning, today we will be reading **Psalm 62:10** (KJV).

> **TRUST NOT IN OPPRESSION, AND BECOME NOT VAIN IN ROBBERY:**
> **IF RICHES INCREASE, SET NOT YOUR HEART UPON THEM.**

And **Psalm 62:10** (NASB)

> **DO NOT TRUST IN OPPRESSION**
> **AND DO NOT VAINLY HOPE IN ROBBERY;**
> **IF RICHES INCREASE, DO NOT SET YOUR HEART UPON THEM.**

And again **Psalm 62:10** (NLT)

> **DON'T MAKE YOUR LIVING BY EXTORTION**
> **OR PUT YOUR HOPE IN STEALING.**
> **AND IF YOUR WEALTH INCREASES,**
> **DON'T MAKE IT THE CENTER OF YOUR LIFE.**

And finally, **Psalm 62:10** (HCSB)

> **PLACE NO TRUST IN OPPRESSION, OR FALSE HOPE IN ROBBERY.**
> **IF WEALTH INCREASES, PAY NO ATTENTION TO IT.**

We cannot be those who chase money by any means possible. And we cannot be those that get wealth at the expense of our brothers and sisters. We value them more than we value ourselves. How could we dishonestly take from them? We love God and love the people, so we seek to bless them. As the Lord does bless us with wealth, it can never have our heart. Wealth can never have our attention, or be the center of our life. Our hearts have been given to our Father; we will not give them to another. We will have no other gods before Him. Now when the wealth comes it can and will be used to serve the kingdom and bless the people. Wealth is simply a tool (like a hammer) to use in building the kingdom. I do not love that hammer, I use it. I do not trust in that hammer, I wield it. And if it does smash my thumb, it was not due to the evil of the hammer but the imprecise way in which I have used it, and the lack of my development in that skill. So I do not curse it and throw it away, I learn to be more precise and I will learn to better develop this skill. It does not consume all my time and attention; it is just one tool of many in my toolbox. So, let's go to work.

We pray the Lord bless you, today.

A Testimony....

One week we heard that our church's school had a window air conditioner stop working in one of the classrooms. The cost was a concern but the real issue was getting a new a/c installed quickly to keep classroom disruption to a minimum.

I knew the Lord wanted us to take care of this for the church, so I asked the pastor if he would let us handle it. I explained that I had installed lots of window a/c's at a job I had during college. I told him we would go get it that day and install it right away. He offered a church check to pay for the unit. But I explained we wanted to take care of everything. He agreed, and you could see one of the many little weights of responsibility lift right off his shoulders.

So, I grabbed the kids and we headed to an appliance store. The a/c was quite a bit more than I expected, but we got a nice one and headed back to church. The install did not go nearly as easily as I expected, either. But by the end of the day, it was installed and working. We did have to come back a few days later and fix some outside trim boards.

I let the pastor and the director of the school know everything was ready for the next school day. It took more money, more time, and more effort than I thought, but it still was our honor to help the kingdom. We were able to use our time, our efforts, our skills, and our money to bless the kingdom, the school, the teachers and students, and our church and pastor. I can't think of a better use of what appears to be mine, than to be used to help others.

I also noticed this simple and really minor act was a not so minor encouragement to the pastor. Just to know he didn't have to bear the weight of everything. Just to know the people were ready, able, and willing to be of help. None of us wants to really be standing out all on our own, and we should not ever have to. This is the Body of Christ and we are members in particular. How great to express our love, our brotherhood, and our oneness with an otherwise trivial thing like money.

We must always be led by the Spirit, but we should also be actively looking and hoping that He will make a way for us to bless someone today.

Testify...

_____
_____
_____
_____
_____
_____

Pray...

_____
_____
_____
_____
_____
_____

Prophesy...

_____
_____
_____
_____

*Blessed be
the God and Father
of our
Lord Jesus Christ,
who has blessed us
with every
spiritual blessing
in the
heavenly places
in Christ,*

Ephesians 1:3 *(NKJV)*

Week #21

Good Morning, today we will be reading Zechariah 1:17 (NKJV).

*"Again proclaim, saying, 'Thus says the Lord of hosts:
"My cities shall again spread out through prosperity;
The Lord will again comfort Zion,
And will again choose Jerusalem."'"*

And Zechariah 1:17 (NASB)
Again, proclaim, saying, 'Thus says the Lord of hosts, "My cities will again overflow with prosperity, and the Lord will again comfort Zion and again choose Jerusalem."'

And Zechariah 1:17 (HCSB)
"Proclaim further: This is what the Lord of Hosts says: My cities will again overflow with prosperity; the Lord will once more comfort Zion and again choose Jerusalem."

And again Zechariah 1:17 (GNT)
The angel also told me to proclaim: "The Lord Almighty says that his cities will be prosperous again and that he will once again help Jerusalem and claim the city as his own."

And finally, Zechariah 1:17 (NLT)
"Say this also: 'This is what the Lord of Heaven's Armies says: The towns of Israel will again overflow with prosperity, and the Lord will again comfort Zion and choose Jerusalem as his own.'"

The children of Israel and Judah had wandered far from God. Their sins were many and they did not deserve the grace and mercy of God. But God sought to bring them back and to bring them home. Not only to bring them out of captivity but also restore what was lost. He did not plan to keep them low and oppressed. He did not seek to make them keep paying for their sins. He wanted to bless them. He wanted to overflow them. He wanted to bless them with such goodness, abundance, and prosperity that they would overflow and expand. The goodness of God is that He comforts us, He chooses us, and He prospers us; when we in no way deserve it. Thank you, our Good, Good Father.

We pray the Lord bless you, today.

A Testimony....

I have a friend who came to my wife and I for some financial advice. As our friend laid out their financial situation, we could see this was about to get very bad for them. They had gotten a used car and the bank loan made their budget very tight. Then they had gotten a bank consolidation loan and now there was no room to breathe in that budget. They had a fixed income and now they had no room for anything (and I mean anything) except the basics and paying those loans.

Normally, the Lord will specifically tell me what to do and how to do it, but this time was different. We wanted to help our friend with advice. But the situation seemed so dire advice really wasn't going to bring any real help, anytime soon. We wanted to help but the situation was so complicated and so big, how could we?

Proverbs 3:27 (NLT) was in the back of my mind for days.
DO NOT WITHHOLD GOOD FROM THOSE WHO DESERVE IT WHEN IT'S IN YOUR POWER TO HELP THEM.

So, my wife and I agreed we would payoff both their loans and then let them pay us back. Now for us, this was no small amount (around $10,000). But we had the money and this was our friend and a child of Almighty God. This would allow our friend to cut their loan payments almost in half and not pay any interest. They could also miss payments if they needed extra money during certain months or seasons. My wife and I also agreed (between us) that we had to be ok with the fact that our friend, in all likelihood, by natural means could never repay this money. But to be a help to our friend, how could that not be worth mere money?

We made arrangements to meet our friend and give them our final "advice." We even learned that things had gotten worse and they were headed to a high-interest loan company just to get enough money to pay their rent. We went over what we wanted to do for them. No more pressure, no more interest, no more razor-thin budgets. It's amazing the difference in people's countenance when they are not under all those weights.

My wife and I were amazed that the goodness of God would give us both the desire and ability to be a help to our friend (**Philippians 2:13**). And only a few months later our friend received a tremendous blessing from the Lord. They were able to set up a savings account, give special gifts to the kingdom, and repay well over half the loan all at once. It is good to be His kids.

Testify...

Pray...

Prophesy...

⁴ just as He chose us in Him before the foundation of the world, that we should be holy and without blame before Him in love, ⁵ having predestined us to adoption as sons by Jesus Christ to Himself, according to the good pleasure of His will, ⁶ to the praise of the glory of His grace, by which He made us accepted in the Beloved.

Ephesians 1:4-6 (NKJV)

Week #22

Good Morning, today we will be reading Matthew 6:24-33 (KJV).

24 NO MAN CAN SERVE TWO MASTERS: FOR EITHER HE WILL HATE THE ONE, AND LOVE THE OTHER; OR ELSE HE WILL HOLD TO THE ONE, AND DESPISE THE OTHER. YE CANNOT SERVE GOD AND MAMMON.
25 THEREFORE I SAY UNTO YOU, TAKE NO THOUGHT FOR YOUR LIFE, WHAT YE SHALL EAT, OR WHAT YE SHALL DRINK; NOR YET FOR YOUR BODY, WHAT YE SHALL PUT ON. IS NOT THE LIFE MORE THAN MEAT, AND THE BODY THAN RAIMENT?
26 BEHOLD THE FOWLS OF THE AIR: FOR THEY SOW NOT, NEITHER DO THEY REAP, NOR GATHER INTO BARNS; YET YOUR HEAVENLY FATHER FEEDETH THEM. ARE YE NOT MUCH BETTER THAN THEY?
27 WHICH OF YOU BY TAKING THOUGHT CAN ADD ONE CUBIT UNTO HIS STATURE?
28 AND WHY TAKE YE THOUGHT FOR RAIMENT? CONSIDER THE LILIES OF THE FIELD, HOW THEY GROW; THEY TOIL NOT, NEITHER DO THEY SPIN:
29 AND YET I SAY UNTO YOU, THAT EVEN SOLOMON IN ALL HIS GLORY WAS NOT ARRAYED LIKE ONE OF THESE.
30 WHEREFORE, IF GOD SO CLOTHE THE GRASS OF THE FIELD, WHICH TO DAY IS, AND TO MORROW IS CAST INTO THE OVEN, SHALL HE NOT MUCH MORE CLOTHE YOU, O YE OF LITTLE FAITH?
31 THEREFORE TAKE NO THOUGHT, SAYING, WHAT SHALL WE EAT? OR, WHAT SHALL WE DRINK? OR, WHEREWITHAL SHALL WE BE CLOTHED?
32 (FOR AFTER ALL THESE THINGS DO THE GENTILES SEEK:) FOR YOUR HEAVENLY FATHER KNOWETH THAT YE HAVE NEED OF ALL THESE THINGS.
33 BUT SEEK YE FIRST THE KINGDOM OF GOD, AND HIS RIGHTEOUSNESS; AND ALL THESE THINGS SHALL BE ADDED UNTO YOU.

And Matthew 6:24 (NLT)
"NO ONE CAN SERVE TWO MASTERS. FOR YOU WILL HATE ONE AND LOVE THE OTHER; YOU WILL BE DEVOTED TO ONE AND DESPISE THE OTHER. YOU CANNOT SERVE GOD AND BE ENSLAVED TO MONEY.

Which do we love? Which one has our attention? Which one really consumes our thoughts? Which one do we plan our life around? We must, "Choose this day, which we will serve... and who or what we will love."

We pray the Lord bless you, today.

A Testimony....

When my son was very young (3-4 years old) we lived in Japan. He became convinced that all escalators (and there were many) were his deadly arch enemies. If I physically held him in my arms, he was fine, but if I tried to just hold his hand, he would still be in terror. Over and over I tried to get him past this fear. We would stand at the bottom of a department store escalator with him crying and me trying to reassure him. I explained this device was meant to help him; it would take him up to the next floor with almost no effort on his part. But still, he was convinced those giant metal teeth had a truly nefarious purpose. I would try and get him to just trust me, his dad. Just to take my hand and I would keep him safe, whether the escalator had good or bad intentions. But still, his tears would stream and he would pull away trying to get some distance from that evil escalator.

Ten years later as I was riding up an escalator in a mall with my son, now a teenager, the Lord brought all that to my remembrance. I explained to him that back then, the very thing we were on now was his greatest fear. It was a world ender, it was panic, fear, and terror. It was life and death, but now it is of no thought at all. It is now a helpful and useful thing. How silly and laughable this story is now many years later. Now that he has grown and developed there is no fear or dread over that metal monster. As my son and I talked about these things, we wondered how all those concerns and challenges that we face today will look years from now. How silly will we feel about all those world-ending monsters we perceive before us today? And why don't we just trust our Father? Whether the monster is real or a paper tiger; if He is with us, then all is well.

Looking back on my perception of being led by the Spirit of God concerning giving, I can see my own childish panic and fear. For well over a decade, I was always so nervous that God would tell me to give "too much". In almost every service, I actively tried not to hear Him concerning the offerings. I just didn't want to hear the Holy Spirit tell me how much to give. I was sure it would be too much. Then I would have to suffer through the consequences during the rest of the week/month.

Now I loved God and trusted Him to lead me in all other areas but I just couldn't take His hand concerning giving. It was in irrational panic and fear that would not let me see the truth. God loves us dearly and He will never hurt us or lead us into hurt if we will just take His hand. The Lord was so patient and kind with me over those years. He didn't yell or scream, He just helped me to grow in Him, in His Word, and in Love. And now because He changed my heart, because of His goodness I can and do trust Him to lead. Now I run to the Spirit to find what I should give, how I should give, when, where, and why I should give. Death and loss never come from His leadings. Life and blessings come both to us and to those to whom we give.

Thank you, Papa.

Testify...

_____
_____
_____
_____
_____
_____
_____

Pray...

_____
_____
_____
_____
_____
_____
_____

Prophesy...

_____
_____
_____
_____
_____
_____

⁷ In Him we have redemption through His blood, the forgiveness of sins, according to the riches of His grace ⁸ which He made to abound toward us in all wisdom and prudence,

Ephesians 1:7-8 (NKJV)

Week #23

Good Morning, today we will be reading **Matthew 6:24-33** (NASB).

24 "No one can serve two masters; for either he will hate the one and love the other, or he will be devoted to one and despise the other. You cannot serve God and wealth.

25 "For this reason I say to you, do not be worried about your life, as to what you will eat or what you will drink; nor for your body, as to what you will put on. Is not life more than food, and the body more than clothing? 26 Look at the birds of the air, that they do not sow, nor reap nor gather into barns, and yet your heavenly Father feeds them. Are you not worth much more than they? 27 And who of you by being worried can add a single hour to his life? 28 And why are you worried about clothing? Observe how the lilies of the field grow; they do not toil nor do they spin, 29 yet I say to you that not even Solomon in all his glory clothed himself like one of these. 30 But if God so clothes the grass of the field, which is alive today and tomorrow is thrown into the furnace, will He not much more clothe you? You of little faith! 31 Do not worry then, saying, 'What will we eat?' or 'What will we drink?' or 'What will we wear for clothing?' 32 For the Gentiles eagerly seek all these things; for your heavenly Father knows that you need all these things. 33 But seek first His kingdom and His righteousness, and all these things will be added to you.

And **Matthew 6:25-26** (NLT)

"That is why I tell you not to worry about everyday life—whether you have enough food and drink, or enough clothes to wear. Isn't life more than food, and your body more than clothing? 26 Look at the birds. They don't plant or harvest or store food in barns, for your heavenly Father feeds them. And aren't you far more valuable to Him than they are?

We need to let go of all our worry, stress, and anxiety over the everyday concerns of life, especially those concerning money. The Father, Our Father, Our Good Father, He knows all that you need, and He has prepared more than enough. You are His most precious child and there is no good thing that He has failed to prepare for you. But we must let Him take the reins. We must turn everything over to Him and let Him lead. You can trust Him; you can put your trust in Him. He will never fail you.

We pray the Lord bless you, today.

A Testimony....

Once when I was driving across lower Kansas in that heroic minivan that God had directed us to buy, God saved me from hitting a deer. Considering only natural and physical aspects that deer should have crashed right through my windshield, but God intervened. The dear was safe and so was I with merely the deer's nose print on one of my side rear windows. It was amazing to see God protect me and that big hunk of metal that rolls me from place to place. My family actively believes and trusts God to protect us and all our vehicles. Then a couple of years later while driving up through northern Kansas, I hit a dear. It had just gotten dark and he ran right out in front of me. It was a 70mph road so even though I slammed on the brakes, we still hit. It was a pretty solid hit, but the deer still ran off. It smashed up my headlight and crumbled my front quarter panel. I asked God, "What was that?"

He showed me a mental picture of a boxer throwing a jab. Ok, I understood He was showing me a picture of my adversary's attack. Then He said, "He drops his left." I could see that jab again and I could see that adversary drop his left hand (his protection against a counterattack). It came racing out of my spirit, if my enemy wants to take a shot at my vehicle then I will give 5 vehicles away.

Over the next many months, we had helped some people with automotive concerns but we hadn't yet been able to give away a vehicle. Then one morning I was awakened by a BOOM! I thought it was a sonic boom until I heard crying outside. It was a neighbor who had accidentally crashed into that minivan. We reassured our distraught neighbor that it was only a vehicle. It was in fact now getting pretty rusty and stacking up the mileage. So, the damage was enough to render it totaled. When I first saw the crashed van, instantly it came out of my spirit, "Ok, now it is ten." Later, when things had settled down, I told my adversary that we would give ten vehicles away and those gifts would lead to the glory of God.

We took the insurance money that we got from that van and blessed two people with it. One who needed help with car payments and one that needed help with car repairs. Not long after we were able to give our first car away. It was not expensive and not anywhere near new, but it was a blessing. I was also present when that family gave glory and honor to God for blessing them with a car. Our enemy never gets to win, we will always continue to give no matter what, for we know in Whom we have believed.

Testify...

Pray...

Prophesy...

⁹ having made known to us the mystery of His will, according to His good pleasure which He purposed in Himself, ¹⁰ that in the dispensation of the fullness of the times He might gather together in one all things in Christ, both which are in heaven and which are on earth—in Him.

Ephesians 1:9-10 (NKJV)

Week #24

Good Morning, today we will be reading Matthew 6:24-33 (HCSB).

24 "NO ONE CAN BE A SLAVE OF TWO MASTERS, SINCE EITHER HE WILL HATE ONE AND LOVE THE OTHER, OR BE DEVOTED TO ONE AND DESPISE THE OTHER. YOU CANNOT BE SLAVES OF GOD AND OF MONEY. 25 "THIS IS WHY I TELL YOU: DON'T WORRY ABOUT YOUR LIFE, WHAT YOU WILL EAT OR WHAT YOU WILL DRINK; OR ABOUT YOUR BODY, WHAT YOU WILL WEAR. ISN'T LIFE MORE THAN FOOD AND THE BODY MORE THAN CLOTHING? 26 LOOK AT THE BIRDS OF THE SKY: THEY DON'T SOW OR REAP OR GATHER INTO BARNS, YET YOUR HEAVENLY FATHER FEEDS THEM. AREN'T YOU WORTH MORE THAN THEY? 27 CAN ANY OF YOU ADD A SINGLE CUBIT TO HIS HEIGHT BY WORRYING? 28 AND WHY DO YOU WORRY ABOUT CLOTHES? LEARN HOW THE WILDFLOWERS OF THE FIELD GROW: THEY DON'T LABOR OR SPIN THREAD. 29 YET I TELL YOU THAT NOT EVEN SOLOMON IN ALL HIS SPLENDOR WAS ADORNED LIKE ONE OF THESE! 30 IF THAT'S HOW GOD CLOTHES THE GRASS OF THE FIELD, WHICH IS HERE TODAY AND THROWN INTO THE FURNACE TOMORROW, WON'T HE DO MUCH MORE FOR YOU—YOU OF LITTLE FAITH? 31 SO DON'T WORRY, SAYING, 'WHAT WILL WE EAT?' OR 'WHAT WILL WE DRINK?' OR 'WHAT WILL WE WEAR?' 32 FOR THE IDOLATERS EAGERLY SEEK ALL THESE THINGS, AND YOUR HEAVENLY FATHER KNOWS THAT YOU NEED THEM. 33 BUT SEEK FIRST THE KINGDOM OF GOD AND HIS RIGHTEOUSNESS, AND ALL THESE THINGS WILL BE PROVIDED FOR YOU.

And Matthew 6:27-33 (NLT)

27 CAN ALL YOUR WORRIES ADD A SINGLE MOMENT TO YOUR LIFE? 28 "AND WHY WORRY ABOUT YOUR CLOTHING? LOOK AT THE LILIES OF THE FIELD AND HOW THEY GROW. THEY DON'T WORK OR MAKE THEIR CLOTHING, 29 YET SOLOMON IN ALL HIS GLORY WAS NOT DRESSED AS BEAUTIFULLY AS THEY ARE. 30 AND IF GOD CARES SO WONDERFULLY FOR WILDFLOWERS THAT ARE HERE TODAY AND THROWN INTO THE FIRE TOMORROW, HE WILL CERTAINLY CARE FOR YOU. WHY DO YOU HAVE SO LITTLE FAITH?
31 "SO DON'T WORRY ABOUT THESE THINGS, SAYING, 'WHAT WILL WE EAT? WHAT WILL WE DRINK? WHAT WILL WE WEAR?' 32 THESE THINGS DOMINATE THE THOUGHTS OF UNBELIEVERS, BUT YOUR HEAVENLY FATHER ALREADY KNOWS ALL YOUR NEEDS. 33 SEEK THE KINGDOM OF GOD ABOVE ALL ELSE, AND LIVE RIGHTEOUSLY, AND HE WILL GIVE YOU EVERYTHING YOU NEED.

Worry can never help you. Being fearful, anxious, and stressed will never change your world. But Faith in your Father can and will change everything. Everything you need is in Him. All good things are available in abundance in the Kingdom. The Goodness of the Kingdom can't be accessed by worry, doubt, or fear. But Faith in the Father grants access to all good things. He knows your needs and has prepared an abundance, seek Him.

We pray the Lord bless you, today.

A Testimony....

Late one winter we learned of a brother in the Lord whose truck had broken down. He didn't think repairing the vehicle was a wise choice considering its age and condition. The Lord ignited in my heart the desire to find a truck to give him. I prayed earnestly that the Lord would let us find a truck for him, before he bought one (craziness considering my original nature).

Within a few weeks, I found a truck coming up for auction, it was a ¾ ton with 4-wheel drive. It was nowhere near new, it had plenty of scratches and dings, but it was still a strong truck. I thought it was a perfect fit for a farm truck for my brother. We were able to get it at auction, and after testing and inspecting it, we agreed it was good enough to give away.

We drove it to church and I asked my brother to come and check out my *new* truck. We could see he liked it so we handed him the keys. There is so much joy in giving (it is amazing that the Father's commands are not grievous, **1 John 5:3**).

Ok, now let me be completely open and honest about this truck. As I was testing it out over about a week or so, I began to really like it. I didn't have a truck like this for my farm; so, why couldn't this be my blessing. It was just a fleeting thing because my love for my brother overwhelmed my selfish thoughts. I also noticed how big and cumbersome that truck was in the city that I lived in most of the time.

Months later I found a midsize truck. It had a strong engine, 4-wheel drive, and enough room for our kids. It was even more perfect for us than the big truck. It was a great blessing. We drove it for a year and then sent it to the farm to serve as an off-road vehicle. Not only did it give me a truck to drive for a year, but it saved me a net of about $4,000 by using it instead of buying an off-road utility vehicle for the farm.

God does all things well. He allowed us to bless our brother, and he blessed us with even greater blessings. And a few weeks later I got a text from that brother, "I love this truck." You just can't get that joy of giving the right gift, without walking hand in hand with the Father. When His Spirit leads, we are definitely headed to many great places.

Testify...

_____
_____
_____
_____
_____
_____

Pray...

_____
_____
_____
_____
_____
_____

Prophesy...

_____
_____
_____
_____
_____

¹³ In Him you also trusted, after you heard the word of truth, the gospel of your salvation; in whom also, having believed, you were sealed with the Holy Spirit of promise, ¹⁴ who is the guarantee of our inheritance until the redemption of the purchased possession, to the praise of His glory.

Ephesians 1:13-14 (NKJV)

Week #25

Good Morning, today we will be reading **Habakkuk 3:17-19** (NLT).

¹⁷ EVEN THOUGH THE FIG TREES HAVE NO BLOSSOMS, AND THERE ARE NO GRAPES ON THE VINES; EVEN THOUGH THE OLIVE CROP FAILS, AND THE FIELDS LIE EMPTY AND BARREN; EVEN THOUGH THE FLOCKS DIE IN THE FIELDS, AND THE CATTLE BARNS ARE EMPTY,
¹⁸ YET I WILL REJOICE IN THE LORD! I WILL BE JOYFUL IN THE GOD OF MY SALVATION!
¹⁹ THE SOVEREIGN LORD IS MY STRENGTH! HE MAKES ME AS SUREFOOTED AS A DEER, ABLE TO TREAD UPON THE HEIGHTS.

And **Habakkuk 3:17-19** (NASB)

¹⁷ THOUGH THE FIG TREE SHOULD NOT BLOSSOM AND THERE BE NO FRUIT ON THE VINES, THOUGH THE YIELD OF THE OLIVE SHOULD FAIL AND THE FIELDS PRODUCE NO FOOD, THOUGH THE FLOCK SHOULD BE CUT OFF FROM THE FOLD AND THERE BE NO CATTLE IN THE STALLS,
¹⁸ YET I WILL EXULT IN THE LORD, I WILL REJOICE IN THE GOD OF MY SALVATION.
¹⁹ THE LORD GOD IS MY STRENGTH, AND HE HAS MADE MY FEET LIKE HINDS' FEET, AND MAKES ME WALK ON MY HIGH PLACES.

And **Habakkuk 3:17-19** (HCSB)

¹⁷ THOUGH THE FIG TREE DOES NOT BUD AND THERE IS NO FRUIT ON THE VINES, THOUGH THE OLIVE CROP FAILS AND THE FIELDS PRODUCE NO FOOD, THOUGH THERE ARE NO SHEEP IN THE PEN AND NO CATTLE IN THE STALLS,
¹⁸ YET I WILL TRIUMPH IN YAHWEH; I WILL REJOICE IN THE GOD OF MY SALVATION!
¹⁹ YAHWEH MY LORD IS MY STRENGTH; HE MAKES MY FEET LIKE THOSE OF A DEER AND ENABLES ME TO WALK ON MOUNTAIN HEIGHTS!

We trust only in our God. We seek only after Him. We rejoice only in Him. His blessing and His abundance are truly wonderful, but we always seek His face, not His hand. We rest in Him.

Let us also read **Habakkuk 3:13** (NRSV).

YOU CAME FORTH TO SAVE YOUR PEOPLE, TO SAVE YOUR ANOINTED. YOU CRUSHED THE HEAD OF THE WICKED HOUSE, LAYING IT BARE FROM FOUNDATION TO ROOF. SELAH

Our salvation, our blessing, and our abundance are in Him, from Him, by Him, and of Him. So we must always keep our focus on our Source. Houses, lands, money, and wealth are wonderful blessings, but they can never be our salvation. They can never be our peace, our joy, or our strength. The Almighty is our God; our eyes are always on Him, and in Him alone do we trust.

We pray the Lord bless you, today.

A Testimony....

I was attending a meeting of a famous preacher when God told me to give away my paycheck. Now, that would have been startling enough on its own, but this was my last paycheck. My company had filed for bankruptcy and I had been let go (ok, fired (man that still stings)). Giving any paycheck away is a real shock to the system, but how could I do this? Of course, we want to hear God and walk in obedience. But my entire paycheck? To make matters even more interesting, my apartment lease was up and the renewal was going to mean a significant rent increase. I had applications in at a few places, but I really wasn't sure even if I got one of those jobs that I could pay all my bills. And now, God wants me to give away the last income I have? I could try and dismiss this leading, but the enemy sure isn't going to tell me to give money into the Kingdom. And my mathematical, budget-driven mind was surely not the one coming up with this idea.

Now, this preacher is a **word of faith** preacher and he is a **prosperity** preacher. Labels and titles that a lot of Christendom shuns away from (would we prefer *word of fear* or *poverty* preachers?). So, was I just caught up in all the hype and excitement? No, I knew this preacher loved God dearly and loved the people. He would never do anything to fleece the children of God. He did challenge us to begin to trust and believe God for hundredfold returns on our giving. **(Mark 10:30 & Genesis 26:12)** It was a battle right up to the time I signed my name to the back of that check. Then joy came, and I was able to place it in that offering with joy and gladness. I was happy that God had brought me to a place and given me the strength to be able to completely trust Him. I was in His hands now.

Neither of my job hopefuls came through but I did get a call from a previous employer. He was also a good friend. I had left that job to move to the city. He called to see how I was doing, and offered me a job. He offered to match what I could make in the city. But small-town living is way less expensive, so it was a very generous offer. I accepted and moved back home. I actually bought a house whose mortgage payment was within a few dollars of being half what I was paying to rent my apartment. The next year while doing my taxes, I was struck by my actual income. I had my base hourly pay, my overtime pay, my sales commissions, and my manufacture's bonuses. All that added up to the entire year's income being just over 100 times that paycheck God had told me to give away. **(1 Kings 17:8-16)**

Testify...

Pray...

Prophesy...

"This God,
our God forever
and ever—
he will always
lead us."

Psalm 48:14 *(CSB)*

Week #26

Good Morning, today we will be reading Psalms 1:1-3 (NRSV).

Happy are those who do not follow the advice of the wicked, or take the path that sinners tread, or sit in the seat of scoffers;
² but their delight is in the law of the Lord, and on his law they meditate day and night.
³ They are like trees planted by streams of water, which yield their fruit in its season, and their leaves do not wither. In all that they do, they prosper.

And Psalms 1:1-3 (NKJV)

Blessed is the man Who walks not in the counsel of the ungodly, Nor stands in the path of sinners, Nor sits in the seat of the scornful;
² But his delight is in the law of the Lord, And in His law he meditates day and night.
³ He shall be like a tree Planted by the rivers of water, That brings forth its fruit in its season, Whose leaf also shall not wither; And whatever he does shall prosper.

And again Psalms 1:1-3 (NLT)

Oh, the joys of those who do not follow the advice of the wicked, or stand around with sinners, or join in with mockers.
² But they delight in the law of the Lord, meditating on it day and night.
³ They are like trees planted along the riverbank, bearing fruit each season. Their leaves never wither, and they prosper in all they do.

And finally, Psalm 1:1-3 (NASB)

How blessed is the man who does not walk in the counsel of the wicked, Nor stand in the path of sinners, Nor sit in the seat of scoffers!
² But his delight is in the law of the Lord, And in His law he meditates day and night.
³ He will be like a tree firmly planted by streams of water, Which yields its fruit in its season And its leaf does not wither; And in whatever he does, he prospers.

When we walk with the Lord, when we hold close to Him and His Word, then we will be steady and true. Then we will grow and abound in fruit. Then we will prosper in those things we set our hands to do. The first things must be first, and they must always be kept first. Our Father wants us to prosper; He just wants us to be in a place to handle that prosperity and not to be handled by it.

We pray the Lord bless you, today.

A Testimony....

While our family lived in Japan, my daughter did some modeling. It was a great way for us to get out into Japan and interact with the people and their culture. We road the Shinkansen and took trips to Osaka and Kyoto. It was very sporadic and more of an adventure than work. But after several years as we were leaving Japan, she had $13,000. Not bad for a kid under 10 years old. I would joke with her how blessed she was and how I was over thirty years old before I had over $10,000 just sitting in a bank account.

When we returned to the U.S. I asked her to consider what she wanted to do with her money. I recommended that she kind of split it into thirds. Save a third for a college starter fund. Save a third so she could by a car when she turned 16. And find a ministry that she loved to give a third into the Kingdom. Almost instantly she replied, "No, I just wanted to give it away." I was quite taken aback. I even tried to reassert my wisdom of saving some for those coming future events (needing a car and paying for college). But no, she had decided to give it all away.

Within a few months, there was a family in need and as the Lord led us, we gave all her money away. Then about six years later, our family found a car for my niece. She wanted a car to replace her truck. She just wanted something that handled better and got better gas mileage. We found and bought the car for her. When we brought it to her, we explained that she could pay us back, whenever she could. There was no hurry or pressure at all. She wanted to give us her truck in exchange for the car. We compared the values of each, and it was a fair deal for her, so we agreed.

I didn't want this truck, because it was a street truck. I have a small farm, so I need a real truck. I want a 4-wheel drive, ¾ ton, 8-foot bed kind of truck that can tow half of the planet. This is a rear-wheel drive, big tires and rims, step side short bed truck. What good would this do for me? But I felt it was the right thing to do for my niece, and we could get some use out of the truck. Turns out my daughter loves this truck. I mean she really *loves* this truck. With all its defects, scratches, dents and dings, she loves this thing. It does have that single cab short bed look that people love to turn into show trucks, so I asked her how much would she take for it if someone wanted to buy it? There is no number, she is not selling that truck.

She trusted God. She used her money to help others, and He blessed her with a perfect truck for her. Not a perfect truck for me, but for her.

I remember as a young driver drooling over those trucks my friends had at school, but there just was no financial way my family could ever afford that. So, I drove an old beater of a truck. Not a classic, not a fixer-upper, a park on a hill so you can pop the clutch to get it started, beater.

It gives me no small amount of joy to see that trusting in God and walking in giving has provided something for my child that I could not have done in my own ability.

Testify...

Pray...

Prophesy...

For you are all children of light, children of the day. We are not of the night or of the darkness.

1 Thessalonians 5:5 *(ESV)*

Week #27

Good Morning, today we will be reading Exodus 36:3-7 (NASB).

³ THEY RECEIVED FROM MOSES ALL THE CONTRIBUTIONS WHICH THE SONS OF ISRAEL HAD BROUGHT TO PERFORM THE WORK IN THE CONSTRUCTION OF THE SANCTUARY. AND THEY STILL CONTINUED BRINGING TO HIM FREEWILL OFFERINGS EVERY MORNING. ⁴ AND ALL THE SKILLFUL MEN WHO WERE PERFORMING ALL THE WORK OF THE SANCTUARY CAME, EACH FROM THE WORK WHICH HE WAS PERFORMING, ⁵ AND THEY SAID TO MOSES, "THE PEOPLE ARE BRINGING MUCH MORE THAN ENOUGH FOR THE CONSTRUCTION WORK WHICH THE LORD COMMANDED US TO PERFORM."
⁶ SO MOSES ISSUED A COMMAND, AND A PROCLAMATION WAS CIRCULATED THROUGHOUT THE CAMP, SAYING, "LET NO MAN OR WOMAN ANY LONGER PERFORM WORK FOR THE CONTRIBUTIONS OF THE SANCTUARY." THUS THE PEOPLE WERE RESTRAINED FROM BRINGING ANY MORE. ⁷ FOR THE MATERIAL THEY HAD WAS SUFFICIENT AND MORE THAN ENOUGH FOR ALL THE WORK, TO PERFORM IT.

And Exodus 36:3-7 (NLT)

³ MOSES GAVE THEM THE MATERIALS DONATED BY THE PEOPLE OF ISRAEL AS SACRED OFFERINGS FOR THE COMPLETION OF THE SANCTUARY. BUT THE PEOPLE CONTINUED TO BRING ADDITIONAL GIFTS EACH MORNING. ⁴ FINALLY THE CRAFTSMEN WHO WERE WORKING ON THE SANCTUARY LEFT THEIR WORK. ⁵ THEY WENT TO MOSES AND REPORTED, "THE PEOPLE HAVE GIVEN MORE THAN ENOUGH MATERIALS TO COMPLETE THE JOB THE LORD HAS COMMANDED US TO DO!"
⁶ SO MOSES GAVE THE COMMAND, AND THIS MESSAGE WAS SENT THROUGHOUT THE CAMP: "MEN AND WOMEN, DON'T PREPARE ANY MORE GIFTS FOR THE SANCTUARY. WE HAVE ENOUGH!" SO THE PEOPLE STOPPED BRINGING THEIR SACRED OFFERINGS. ⁷ THEIR CONTRIBUTIONS WERE MORE THAN ENOUGH TO COMPLETE THE WHOLE PROJECT.

Let us also read **Exodus 35:21, 29** (HCSB).

²¹ EVERYONE WHOSE HEART WAS MOVED AND WHOSE SPIRIT PROMPTED HIM CAME AND BROUGHT AN OFFERING TO THE LORD FOR THE WORK ON THE TENT OF MEETING, FOR ALL ITS SERVICES, AND FOR THE HOLY GARMENTS.
²⁹ SO THE ISRAELITES BROUGHT A FREEWILL OFFERING TO THE LORD, ALL THE MEN AND WOMEN WHOSE HEARTS PROMPTED THEM TO BRING SOMETHING FOR ALL THE WORK THAT THE LORD, THROUGH MOSES, HAD COMMANDED TO BE DONE.

When we will listen to His Spirit and be led and inspired by Him, there will never be a need to beg the people to support the work of the kingdom. It will be unthinkable to push, prod, or coerce the people into giving to the work of the Lord. When we are led by the Spirit, there will always be more than enough in the House of God to do the work of the kingdom. We the people need to learn to run to the Spirit, trusting in Him in full faith. We shall be blessed and the work of the kingdom will overflow with abundance.

We pray the Lord bless you, today.

A Testimony....

I remember as a kid growing up in small churches. They were great for those things considered *spiritual*. The teaching, preaching, praise and worship, the signs and wonders, and the precious moving and workings of the Holy Spirit were all more than we could have hoped for from such small groups of believers. But the one seemingly constant issue was finances. We could seem to only barely pay the bills; we could feed the pastor but it wasn't steak and lobster. And if a special need arose or a repair was needed for the church, we were really scrambling. I can remember multiple offerings over weeks and months just to cover those unexpected expenses. I can even remember multiple offerings, in the same service, for the same need, because of the urgency and the first offering was just not enough.

We had great revelation on many wonderful things in the Kingdom, but concerning money, we seemed stuck. We believed in being led by the Spirit of God in your daily walk, but concerning money, we had to follow the rules and regulations. We believed in the merciful grace of God, but if you didn't give, that same God was ready to drop that big hammer. Religion never leads to the blessings of God. Fear and regulation never lead to a free walk with the Father.

I rejoice so much that He has led us through those things and shown us how to be led by His Spirit and how to walk free in Him.

Many decades later, during one service the Lord showed me a wonderful scene. The church announcing a need and like popcorn people jumping up to say they would take care of the need. It was an excited, joyful, rush among the people. Like, "pick me, pick me!" They were hopeful that the pastor would pick them among all the others in the church standing and waiting to meet this need. I saw an interesting look on the pastor's face, now he had to decide who among so many would get the responsibility and honor.

It was a wonderful scene and I relayed it to the pastor later. I suggested some wisdom in being ready to divide up the task to let many participate. Now, this is may not be what we currently see, but it is what we can see by faith. It is what we shall soon behold, as the Spirit continues to bless us and grow us in our walk with Him.

Not long after it was announced that the church building's side door needed to be replaced. The Spirit ignited my heart, and I rushed to the pastor after service and asked if I could please be the one to take care of this project. The Kingdom is worth our excitement, our time, our money, and our putting it first.

Testify...

Pray...

Prophesy...

⁶ Having then gifts differing according to the grace that is given to us, let us use them: if prophecy, let us prophesy in proportion to our faith; ⁷ or ministry, let us use it in our ministering; he who teaches, in teaching; ⁸ he who exhorts, in exhortation; he who gives, with liberality; he who leads, with diligence; he who shows mercy, with cheerfulness.

Romans 12:6-8 (NKJV)

Week #28

Good Morning, today we will be reading **Philippians 4:19** (ESV).

AND MY GOD WILL SUPPLY EVERY NEED OF YOURS ACCORDING TO HIS RICHES IN GLORY IN CHRIST JESUS.

And **Philippians 4:19** (NLT)

AND THIS SAME GOD WHO TAKES CARE OF ME WILL SUPPLY ALL YOUR NEEDS FROM HIS GLORIOUS RICHES, WHICH HAVE BEEN GIVEN TO US IN CHRIST JESUS.

And again **Philippians 4:19** (NASB)

AND MY GOD WILL SUPPLY ALL YOUR NEEDS ACCORDING TO HIS RICHES IN GLORY IN CHRIST JESUS.

This is an amazing promise filled with wonder and awe. That God would meet our needs, and that He would meet them not based on our era, nation, or socioeconomic class; but according to His ability, His abundance, and His riches. But to whom was this promise made?

Let us read the previous four verses **Philippians 4:15-18** (ESV).

¹⁵ AND YOU PHILIPPIANS YOURSELVES KNOW THAT IN THE BEGINNING OF THE GOSPEL, WHEN I LEFT MACEDONIA, NO CHURCH ENTERED INTO PARTNERSHIP WITH ME IN GIVING AND RECEIVING, EXCEPT YOU ONLY. ¹⁶ EVEN IN THESSALONICA YOU SENT ME HELP FOR MY NEEDS ONCE AND AGAIN. ¹⁷ NOT THAT I SEEK THE GIFT, BUT I SEEK THE FRUIT THAT INCREASES TO YOUR CREDIT. ¹⁸ I HAVE RECEIVED FULL PAYMENT, AND MORE. I AM WELL SUPPLIED, HAVING RECEIVED FROM EPAPHRODITUS THE GIFTS YOU SENT, A FRAGRANT OFFERING, A SACRIFICE ACCEPTABLE AND PLEASING TO GOD.

And **Philippians 4:15-18** (HCSB)

¹⁵ AND YOU PHILIPPIANS KNOW THAT IN THE EARLY DAYS OF THE GOSPEL, WHEN I LEFT MACEDONIA, NO CHURCH SHARED WITH ME IN THE MATTER OF GIVING AND RECEIVING EXCEPT YOU ALONE. ¹⁶ FOR EVEN IN THESSALONICA YOU SENT GIFTS FOR MY NEED SEVERAL TIMES. ¹⁷ NOT THAT I SEEK THE GIFT, BUT I SEEK THE PROFIT THAT IS INCREASING TO YOUR ACCOUNT. ¹⁸ BUT I HAVE RECEIVED EVERYTHING IN FULL, AND I HAVE AN ABUNDANCE. I AM FULLY SUPPLIED, HAVING RECEIVED FROM EPAPHRODITUS WHAT YOU PROVIDED—A FRAGRANT OFFERING, AN ACCEPTABLE SACRIFICE, PLEASING TO GOD.

Here we see the ones to whom the promise is made. Those that love and support the kingdom. Those whose faith in God has moved them to help send the gospel of Christ to all the world. Our faith should move us to act. Our trust in the Father releases us from the worry, the stress, and the worldly concerns about money. We know our Father has and will always provide, abundantly for us, so now we are free to give. And that very faith is what opens wide the doors for the Father to move on our behalf.

We pray the Lord bless you, today.

A Testimony....

Each year my family attends a week-long church convention. I started attending this event long before I even had a family. I used to drive down alone and I really didn't have much. I would eat as cheaply as I could. One year my mom baked a few loaves of bread and they were the majority of my food for many days. I stayed in the cheapest hotels I could find, that was always let's just say "interesting."

Each year I went with the main purpose of learning more and more about God. But I was also hoping that God would bless me financially, somehow and some way. Years and years went by. I learned so much and developed a deeper and deeper walk with God through those meetings, but never did I see a big financial blessing.

Over the years I even let that hope and expectation fade away. Then the Lord changed my outlook. I began to look around and expectantly look for someone that the Lord would allow me to bless. I let go of looking out for a blessing for myself and I endeavored to be a blessing. I now set out with purpose (joyfully) to bring an offering to be a help to those meetings.

Now over 20 years from those beginnings, I can look around and see the abundant blessing of God. Now I am not just one, I am a family. It's not just me attending this convention but my wife, my two kids, and I. So, one has become four.

Now, we eat what we what and where we want. There is plenty, and I no longer have to count the cost. Mind you we are not eating at four-star restaurants, but we choose where we want to eat. It is no longer dictated to us based on price and budget.

We also stay in hotels that we choose. No longer those very "interesting" places that require a lot of faith just to rest easy. Again, we don't stay at the five-star hotels in the heart of downtown but we stay in hotels that we like. We get to choose and that is a very liberating thing. We are not subject to money, but it is subject to us.

I was musing about the stark contrast and telling old stories to my son at the last convention. God never sent me any gold bricks and no one ever mailed me a $100,000 check. But I can look all around and see the blessing of the Lord. He has set the lonely in families **(Psalms 68:6)**. Nothing quite seemed to work well when money was a *concern*. But when I learn to rest in Him by faith, everything began to change And He has freed us from being subject to money. Now, we are free to use it. We are free to seek the Kingdom first, bless others, and to live well.

Testify...

Pray...

Prophesy...

⁹ Let love be without hypocrisy. Abhor what is evil. Cling to what is good. ¹⁰ Be kindly affectionate to one another with brotherly love, in honor giving preference to one another;

Romans 12:9-10 (NKJV)

Week #29

Good Morning, today we will be reading the 23rd Psalm (NKJV).

¹ The Lord is my shepherd; I shall not want. ² He makes me to lie down in green pastures; He leads me beside the still waters. ³ He restores my soul; He leads me in the paths of righteousness For His name's sake. ⁴ Yea, though I walk through the valley of the shadow of death, I will fear no evil; For You are with me; Your rod and Your staff, they comfort me. ⁵ You prepare a table before me in the presence of my enemies; You anoint my head with oil; My cup runs over. ⁶ Surely goodness and mercy shall follow me All the days of my life; And I will dwell in the house of the Lord Forever.

And the 23rd Psalm (HCSB)

¹ The Lord is my shepherd; there is nothing I lack. ² He lets me lie down in green pastures; He leads me beside quiet waters. ³ He renews my life; He leads me along the right paths for His name's sake. ⁴ Even when I go through the darkest valley, I fear no danger, for You are with me; Your rod and Your staff—they comfort me. ⁵ You prepare a table before me in the presence of my enemies; You anoint my head with oil; my cup overflows. ⁶ Only goodness and faithful love will pursue me all the days of my life, and I will dwell in the house of the Lord as long as I live.

And finally, the 23rd Psalm (NASB)

¹ The Lord is my shepherd, I shall not want. ² He makes me lie down in green pastures; He leads me beside quiet waters. ³ He restores my soul; He guides me in the paths of righteousness For His name's sake. ⁴ Even though I walk through the valley of the shadow of death, I fear no evil, for You are with me; Your rod and Your staff, they comfort me. ⁵ You prepare a table before me in the presence of my enemies; You have anointed my head with oil; My cup overflows. ⁶ Surely goodness and lovingkindness will follow me all the days of my life, And I will dwell in the house of the Lord forever.

God wants to satisfy you to the point where you have no more wants. He just has to get your wants to the place where they are not things that will hurt you or others. Once you are letting Him lead, letting Him shepherd you, then you can have that overflowing cup. You will have more than enough, and you will eagerly be seeking someone to bless with all that overflow.

We pray the Lord bless you, today.

A Testimony....

Let me tell of the leadings and guiding of the Lord that kept me in just the right place to receive a nice blessing. Our washer on the farm had been banging and dancing all over the place during the start of the spin cycle. We repaired it a couple of months ago, but that repair only lasted several weeks before it went back to its raucous ways. I reordered new parts and was set to repair it again. But in checking it over we realized that the parts we put on had not failed. So, these new parts would make no difference. I decided that I could upgrade the original design, and maybe that would settle this wild child down. I just needed a few more parts to try my upgrade.

I was in town so I went by the local hardware store. The owner helped me find what I needed and then sent me over to the counter to check out. He told the young man what to ring up, but I noticed he said 4 eye bolts when I actually had 5. So, I asked the young man to ring up one more. Doing what was right, is right, no matter the extra cost... 69 cents. That was the cost of being honest and walking like my Father. I know it is a small thing, but small things matter. Small things reveal your heart and set you on a path (good or bad).

Well, my repair met with very limited success both in effectiveness and in duration. I knew what I should do, go and buy a new machine, but... This machine was not that old and had not been used that much. And in about a year, we would be moving everything from our Nebraska home to the farm. Then we would have two, too many washers. So, couldn't we just deal with this one until then? No, I knew in my spirit what was right. Ok, ok but couldn't I just find a used one or take some time to find a really great deal? No, my mother who lives on the farm was recovering from minor surgery and it was not right to have her deal with this defective machine. She is a daughter of Almighty God and having a semi-weekly wrestling match with a rebellious washer that keeps trying to walk out the back door is not what she is called to do.

We headed to the store *(now small things matter)*. I wanted to buy it online and just pick it up at the store, but the Spirit said no. I wanted to go by the two other stores I needed to go to first (because they closed first) but the Spirit said no, first things first. At the store in the appliance section, we saw that there was a $50 rebate for picking up the machine (we would never have known, had we bought online and only went to the service desk to pick it up.)

I also have a card that gets me a 10% discount from this store. The machine was $699 but on sale for $629 then my discount should save me an extra $63. But I knew I should not use or show this card. Logic and reason were making some pretty good arguments but I knew what the Lord wanted me to do (and not do).

Is it logic and reason that I am led by, or am I led by God (now, they don't have to be mutually exclusive, but when they head in opposite directions who do I follow)? When my wisdom and my knowledge show one path and my Father shows another, which will I choose? Do I really believe that He is; and that He is a rewarder of those that diligently seek Him **(Hebrews 11:6)**? My actions will reveal my faith **(James 2:14-26)**. Thank God, for His Spirit to empower me both to will and to do **(Philippians 2:13)**.

I didn't use my card, but when I give them my phone number, they will see my account and give me the discount anyway (so, I thought). But, no. So, we headed to check out. Even there came a choice to jump into a newly opened register line, or do what was right and let those who were waiting in line take those spots. By His grace, we remained true to what was right. At the register, my brain wanted to let that card in my wallet show and let the checker discover it and give me that discount. But the Spirit would not budge and so I put that card face down.

As I went to pay, I realized the price couldn't be right. It was $547. It doesn't take very many math degrees to realize if the item is on sale for $629 plus tax then a $547 total is not correct. I told the checker that can't be correct. We checked the make and model number, everything was correct. It was the right price. So, we paid rather joyfully and loaded the machine. We later read the receipt and it said, "minimum retail price applied to this item."

God had arranged a blessing. My discount would have been $63, but His discount was $130. He doubled what I could have done, and added an additional $50 rebate on top of that. Doing what is right no matter the cost, keeps us in line with the blessing. Walking by faith according to His leading keeps us in just the right place to receive all His gifts. This is not a works thing, or a judgment thing, it is a choice to trust and believe Him, or not.

Even as children of God, we still choose each day and in all areas of our life if we will follow Him. He is our Savior, is He our Lord? He loves us so much and has designed good things for us. Walking with our Lord will never lead to a less than life.

He has shown you, O man, what is good; And what does the Lord require of you

Testify...

_____
_____
_____
_____

Pray...

_____
_____
_____
_____

Prophesy...

_____
_____
_____
_____

But to do justly, To love mercy, And to walk humbly with your God?

Micah 6:8 *(NKJV)*

Week #30

Good Morning, today we will be reading **Habakkuk 3:17-19** (NASB).

¹⁷ Though the fig tree should not blossom And there be no fruit on the vines, Though the yield of the olive should fail And the fields produce no food, Though the flock should be cut off from the fold And there be no cattle in the stalls, ¹⁸ Yet I will exult in the Lord, I will rejoice in the God of my salvation. ¹⁹ The Lord God is my strength, And He has made my feet like hinds' feet, And makes me walk on my high places.

And **Habakkuk 3:17-19** (NKJV)

¹⁷ Though the fig tree may not blossom, Nor fruit be on the vines; Though the labor of the olive may fail, And the fields yield no food; Though the flock may be cut off from the fold, And there be no herd in the stalls— ¹⁸ Yet I will rejoice in the Lord, I will joy in the God of my salvation. ¹⁹ The Lord God is my strength; He will make my feet like deer's feet, And He will make me walk on my high hills.

And again **Habakkuk 3:17-19** (NLT)

¹⁷ Even though the fig trees have no blossoms, and there are no grapes on the vines; even though the olive crop fails, and the fields lie empty and barren; even though the flocks die in the fields, and the cattle barns are empty, ¹⁸ yet I will rejoice in the Lord! I will be joyful in the God of my salvation! ¹⁹ The Sovereign Lord is my strength! He makes me as surefooted as a deer, able to tread upon the heights.

And finally, **Habakkuk 3:17-19** (NIV)

¹⁷ Though the fig tree does not bud and there are no grapes on the vines, though the olive crop fails and the fields produce no food, though there are no sheep in the pen and no cattle in the stalls, ¹⁸ yet I will rejoice in the Lord, I will be joyful in God my Savior. ¹⁹ The Sovereign Lord is my strength; he makes my feet like the feet of a deer, he enables me to tread on the heights.

Our strength is not in our finances. Our strength is not in our great possessions. Our strength is in our Lord, He never falls short. Our salvation is never found in our accounts. Our savings is not our Savior. Our 401k will never contain our salvation. We should never confuse our blessings with THE Blessing. No matter the size of our salary or wage, we will rejoice in Him. No matter whether bull or bear, our strength is in Him. Recession or contraction, we will not stumble or fall; because He has set out the path and strengthened our abilities. Our position is set by the Lord our God and we rejoice in Him. Oh, how we rejoice in Him.

We pray the Lord bless you, today.

A Testimony....

This is a testimony that my mother has about the provision of God. Our family had moved from Oklahoma to Ohio. The oil bust in Oklahoma had made work and finances *extremely* difficult. We had moved to Ohio in the hope of better things. It took everything we had to get there. So when we got to Ohio, we had no money, no furniture, no refrigerator, etc.

One day there was nothing to eat and no money for food. My mother did have a jar of spaghetti sauce. She also found a few strands of spaghetti noodles in an emptied out package. She filled up a big pot with water and set it to boil. She put those few strands of noodles into the pot and said, "God, you have to feed my babies."

When the spaghetti was finished cooking there was plenty of spaghetti in that pot. My sisters and I ate until we were full, and then there wasn't anymore.

God had provided where there was no provision.

Then over the next few days, people just kept coming to our house. Some with food, some with furniture, and even someone with a refrigerator.

Should we not call on our Father when we are in need? Is He not the Almighty God? Is He not known as Jehovah Jireh - the LORD our provider?

> **FOR "WHOEVER WILL CALL ON THE NAME OF THE LORD WILL BE SAVED."**
>
> Romans 10:13 (NASB)

Saved from sin and death, yes. Saved from sickness and disease, yes. Saved from hunger, lack, and poverty, yes.

Saved – sozo – to save, heal, preserve, and rescue. (Strong's 4982)

To be whole, to be complete – nothing missing, nothing broken - *Shalom*

Testify...

_____
_____
_____
_____
_____
_____
_____

Pray...

_____
_____
_____
_____
_____
_____
_____

Prophesy...

_____
_____
_____
_____
_____

¹¹ not lagging in diligence, fervent in spirit, serving the Lord; ¹² rejoicing in hope, patient in tribulation, continuing steadfastly in prayer; ¹³ distributing to the needs of the saints, given to hospitality

Romans 12:11-13 (NKJV)

Week #31

Good Morning, today we will be reading **Haggai 2:18-19** (NASB).

¹⁸ 'Do consider from this day onward, from the twenty-fourth day of the ninth month; from the day when the temple of the Lord was founded, consider: ¹⁹ Is the seed still in the barn? Even including the vine, the fig tree, the pomegranate and the olive tree, it has not borne fruit. Yet from this day on I will bless you.'"

And **Haggai 2:18-19** (NLT)

¹⁸ "Think about this eighteenth day of December, the day when the foundation of the Lord's Temple was laid. Think carefully. ¹⁹ I am giving you a promise now while the seed is still in the barn. You have not yet harvested your grain, and your grapevines, fig trees, pomegranates, and olive trees have not yet produced their crops. But from this day onward I will bless you."

And again **Haggai 2:18-19** (NIV)

¹⁸ 'From this day on, from this twenty-fourth day of the ninth month, give careful thought to the day when the foundation of the Lord's temple was laid. Give careful thought: ¹⁹ Is there yet any seed left in the barn? Until now, the vine and the fig tree, the pomegranate and the olive tree have not borne fruit.
"'From this day on I will bless you.'"

The people of God had gotten so busy taking care of themselves that they neglected the House of God. And they never seemed to have enough. The harvests were never abundant and what was harvested never lasted.

Let us also read **Haggai 2:15-16** (NLT).

¹⁵ Look at what was happening to you before you began to lay the foundation of the Lord's Temple. ¹⁶ When you hoped for a twenty-bushel crop, you harvested only ten. When you expected to draw fifty gallons from the winepress, you found only twenty.

We never seem to do very well on our own. We never seem to be as smart, strong, and clever as we think we are. Our plans falter and fail. The pillars of our strength crack and crumble to dust. But when we run to our Father God, when we run to His plan and His strength, then those blessings come. When we let go of the stress, the efforts, and the control, and when we do this by Faith then our God can move. Oh, how the Father wants to bless His children, we just need to run to His House, run home to His arms. Then mark it on the calendar, pay attention, because His blessing does not fall short, His blessing is Abundance. Pressed down shaken together and running over Abundance.

We pray the Lord bless you, today.

A Testimony....

One year a brother in the Lord began to have some vehicle repair issues, eventually bringing his family down to one vehicle. Since his wife worked in the evening he was not able to attend Wednesday night service. They were saving for another vehicle but I truly missed him and his family at church. With the vehicles we had, there was just no feasible way to get him and his four small children to church.

I prayed and asked God to please let me help him in some way. Then one day while working away at my computer, I paused and opened an auction site that I use. I didn't need anything, but I just had an unction to go to that site. Sure enough, they had a minivan up for auction that would allow me to take him and his kids to church. I was quite busy that day, so I put in my bid $1,000, and went back to work. I prayed that God would help that bid stand. By all natural and reasonable means that should not have been the winning bid. Normally, I would watch the bidding down to the last second but I endeavored to let Him work on my behalf.

I actually got so caught up in work that I forgot about the time and it was well past the close of the auction when I went to check the results. I had won, the $1,000 bid had stood. This van was nearly identical to my heroic van that had been crumpled, except it had over 80 thousand fewer miles. It was almost like going back in time nearly 5 years to when we bought that original van, expect this one was nearly 1/8 the price. Well for many months we got to take our brother to church on Wednesday nights. Even those trips across town were a blessing of fellowship, as we talked about God, listened to some great teachers, and listened to many praises of God.

Later that year his wife's schedule was changed and they were able to attend as a family again. And within about a week, we started to have issues with the van. Its purpose had been fulfilled, and I didn't feel comfortable giving it away with it having "issues." So I decided to scrap it, but God told me to repair it. He walked me through one issue after another. It was strange, but I enjoyed working on it (which is not normally the case). Step by step God led me to repair it, piece by piece. Several times I wanted to just give up but God kept me on course. Soon all the repairs were done, and it ran great. It has made multiple 1,000 plus mile trips back and forth to our farm. It has hauled trailers with equipment and is turning into another heroic van. We have been so blessed, and all because we simply wanted to be a blessing.

Testify...

Pray...

Prophesy...

¹⁴ Bless those who persecute you; bless and do not curse. ¹⁵ Rejoice with those who rejoice, and weep with those who weep. ¹⁶ Be of the same mind toward one another. Do not set your mind on high things, but associate with the humble. Do not be wise in your own opinion.

Romans 12:14-16 (NKJV)

Week #32

Good Morning, today we will be reading **1 Corinthians 16:1-3** (NLT).

¹ Now regarding your question about the money being collected for God's people in Jerusalem. You should follow the same procedure I gave to the churches in Galatia. ² On the first day of each week, you should each put aside a portion of the money you have earned. Don't wait until I get there and then try to collect it all at once. ³ When I come, I will write letters of recommendation for the messengers you choose to deliver your gift to Jerusalem.

And **1 Corinthians 16:1-3** (HCSB)

¹ Now about the collection for the saints: You should do the same as I instructed the Galatian churches. ² On the first day of the week, each of you is to set something aside and save in keeping with how he prospers, so that no collections will need to be made when I come. ³ When I arrive, I will send with letters those you recommend to carry your gracious gift to Jerusalem.

And again **1 Corinthians 16:1-3** (NKJV)

¹ Now concerning the collection for the saints, as I have given orders to the churches of Galatia, so you must do also: ² On the first day of the week let each one of you lay something aside, storing up as he may prosper, that there be no collections when I come. ³ And when I come, whomever you approve by your letters I will send to bear your gift to Jerusalem.

Our giving should be dedicated and done with purpose. We should not be scrambling to grab something at the last minute. We should not be pushed or manipulated into gifting. We give to bless our brothers and sisters and further the Kingdom. We give as we are led by His Spirit. Our giving comes from that deep abiding love that God has sown into our hearts when we came back to Him.

Let us look at a few more verses from later in that same chapter.

¹³ Watch, stand fast in the faith, be bold like men, and be strong. ¹⁴ Let all that you do be done with love.

1 Corinthians 16:13-14 (MEV)

Our giving is not based on numbers, statistics, or financial projections. Our giving is based on our faith in God. God has us and has provided all we need. Now we are free to give. We are free to express our love, through our giving.

We pray the Lord bless you, today.

A Testimony....

I have mentioned in a previous testimony how we had a real financial decision to make when my family was moving to Japan. Should we cut off our giving until we could re-establish ourselves? Our income was getting cut in half so my logic and my budget were screaming at me to pause all our giving just until we could see how things would work out. But thanks be to God that He had changed my old miserly heart and allowed me to love the Kingdom more than myself. We trusted in God, we counted on Him to take care of us, not our income. As I have already told He did bless our family greatly.

One day I went to the bank to exchange some currency. My daughter had been so blessed that we already had too much yen and had to put some away. As the bank teller processed our transaction, she looked back at the screen and asked if we were interested in a CD (Certificate of Deposit). We had been living on my wife's paycheck for a couple of years, but now I was also working. So, my paycheck was just going straight into the bank. The account was starting to grow, and that was what the teller noticed.

I explained to the teller that we wanted to keep our money liquid as we were actively looking to buy property back home and we needed our funds readily available. So, I politely declined and headed out toward the lobby. As I got to those lobby doors, it hit me what just happened. I began praising God in English and in tongues. They had just asked to borrow money from us. The bank had asked to borrow our money, and pay us interest for using *our* money (essentially that's what a CD is).

The borrower had become the lender... God's word had manifested itself in our everyday life.

[11] THE LORD WILL MAKE YOU PROSPER ABUNDANTLY WITH CHILDREN, THE OFFSPRING OF YOUR LIVESTOCK, AND YOUR LAND'S PRODUCE IN THE LAND THE LORD SWORE TO YOUR FATHERS TO GIVE YOU. [12] THE LORD WILL OPEN FOR YOU HIS ABUNDANT STOREHOUSE, THE SKY, TO GIVE YOUR LAND RAIN IN ITS SEASON AND TO BLESS ALL THE WORK OF YOUR HANDS. YOU WILL LEND TO MANY NATIONS, BUT YOU WILL NOT BORROW. [13] THE LORD WILL MAKE YOU THE HEAD AND NOT THE TAIL; YOU WILL ONLY MOVE UPWARD AND NEVER DOWNWARD IF YOU LISTEN TO THE LORD YOUR GOD'S COMMANDS I AM GIVING YOU TODAY AND ARE CAREFUL TO FOLLOW THEM. [14] DO NOT TURN ASIDE TO THE RIGHT OR THE LEFT FROM ALL THE THINGS I AM COMMANDING YOU TODAY, AND DO NOT GO AFTER OTHER GODS TO WORSHIP THEM.

Deuteronomy 28:11-14 (HCSB)

Testify...

Pray...

Prophesy...

¹⁷ Repay no one evil for evil. Have regard for good things in the sight of all men. ¹⁸ If it is possible, as much as depends on you, live peaceably with all men.

Romans 12:17-18 (NKJV)

Week #33

Good Morning, today we will be reading **1 Corinthians 13:1-8a** (MEV).

¹ IF I SPEAK WITH THE TONGUES OF MEN AND OF ANGELS, AND HAVE NOT LOVE, I HAVE BECOME AS SOUNDING BRASS OR A CLANGING CYMBAL. ² IF I HAVE THE GIFT OF PROPHECY, AND UNDERSTAND ALL MYSTERIES AND ALL KNOWLEDGE, AND IF I HAVE ALL FAITH, SO THAT I COULD REMOVE MOUNTAINS, AND HAVE NOT LOVE, I AM NOTHING. ³ IF I GIVE ALL MY GOODS TO FEED THE POOR, AND IF I GIVE MY BODY TO BE BURNED, AND HAVE NOT LOVE, IT PROFITS ME NOTHING. ⁴ LOVE SUFFERS LONG AND IS KIND; LOVE ENVIES NOT; LOVE FLAUNTS NOT ITSELF AND IS NOT PUFFED UP, ⁵ DOES NOT BEHAVE ITSELF IMPROPERLY, SEEKS NOT ITS OWN, IS NOT EASILY PROVOKED, THINKS NO EVIL; ⁶ REJOICES NOT IN INIQUITY, BUT REJOICES IN THE TRUTH; ⁷ BEARS ALL THINGS, BELIEVES ALL THINGS, HOPES ALL THINGS, AND ENDURES ALL THINGS. ⁸ LOVE NEVER FAILS.

And **1 Corinthians 13:3** (NKJV)

³ AND THOUGH I BESTOW ALL MY GOODS TO FEED THE POOR, AND THOUGH I GIVE MY BODY TO BE BURNED, BUT HAVE NOT LOVE, IT PROFITS ME NOTHING.

And **1 Corinthians 13:3** (NASB)

³ AND IF I GIVE ALL MY POSSESSIONS TO FEED THE POOR, AND IF I SURRENDER MY BODY TO BE BURNED, BUT DO NOT HAVE LOVE, IT PROFITS ME NOTHING.

And finally, **1 Corinthians 13:3-7** (NLT)

³ IF I GAVE EVERYTHING I HAVE TO THE POOR AND EVEN SACRIFICED MY BODY, I COULD BOAST ABOUT IT; BUT IF I DIDN'T LOVE OTHERS, I WOULD HAVE GAINED NOTHING. ⁴ LOVE IS PATIENT AND KIND. LOVE IS NOT JEALOUS OR BOASTFUL OR PROUD ⁵ OR RUDE. IT DOES NOT DEMAND ITS OWN WAY. IT IS NOT IRRITABLE, AND IT KEEPS NO RECORD OF BEING WRONGED. ⁶ IT DOES NOT REJOICE ABOUT INJUSTICE BUT REJOICES WHENEVER THE TRUTH WINS OUT. ⁷ LOVE NEVER GIVES UP, NEVER LOSES FAITH, IS ALWAYS HOPEFUL, AND ENDURES THROUGH EVERY CIRCUMSTANCE.

Our heart matters. Our motivation matters. Why we do what we do matters. Do we give out of fear? Do we give as a religious practice? Do we give because we are required to, or so that *we* will feel good? When we give, is it about us or about them? We must search our hearts and if they are not right, then we must run to God because only He can change us. We want a heart like God, we want to love like God. We want to never give up, never lose faith, always be hopeful, always endure, and we want our life to be about them and not about us. We want all our giving to come from this heart of love.

We pray the Lord bless you, today.

A Testimony....

I have a friend whose mother needed a washing machine. He had given up many things to serve directly in kingdom work. The Lord told us to buy a washer for his mother on his behalf. The Lord said to tell him that just because he had given up more seemingly lucrative opportunities to serve God, did not mean that he would miss out on the joys of helping his family. God's benefits and rewards are always so much better than any Fortune 500 company could ever imagine.

We had talked to my friend and agreed to get the washer on a certain day. The morning of that day my daughter called me from school. She had noticed all the loose coins from her truck were gone and her wallet had been gone through. She asked if her mother or I had been in her truck. We hadn't and so I went out to check my van. It also was missing all its loose change, and a few hundred dollars that were in my jacket pocket was gone as well. We did not as a habit lock our vehicles that are parked in our driveway. Someone had gotten into those two vehicles and had taken any money they could find.

When my daughter got home, I sat her down to talk about all this. I was concerned about her heart and any anger or vengefulness she might have concerning this violation. But she was deeply concerned for the thief. She was concerned for the state this person must be in to do such a thing. We talked about these things and also about the trouble this thief was in because he had robbed children of God. So, we prayed. We prayed that God would forgive this person (they had no idea who they had robbed and what those consequences were - **Luke 23:34** & **Acts 7:60**). We also prayed that the Holy Spirit would lead them to the saving knowledge of Jesus.

Our hearts were good, but my head was running numbers. We had just lost a few hundred dollars, maybe we should hold off on this washer thing. But love prevails. I so wanted to bless my friend so that he could have the joy of helping his mother. Love prevails over logic, reason, and budgets. I headed off to the store to pick up that washer.

There was another heart issue that day. There was a bible study at my friend's mom's house later that night. So, if I brought it at just the right time, everyone would see this good work of mine. But of course, God said no. He was protecting my heart, my gift, and my blessing. My friend had said that he would be off work in time to install the washer long before the bible study. This way it would be done and not interfere with the study. Also, this let him be the one to bring this blessing to his mom, which was the point anyway. My ego, pride, and flesh might not have liked this; but my spirit sure could see the beauty of how God works out all things well.

Our hearts are precious and we should guard them well.

WATCH OVER YOUR HEART WITH ALL DILIGENCE, FOR FROM IT *FLOW* THE SPRINGS OF LIFE. Proverbs 4:23 (NASB)

Testify...

_____
_____
_____
_____
_____
_____
_____

Pray...

_____
_____
_____
_____
_____
_____
_____

Prophesy...

_____
_____
_____
_____
_____

Do not be overcome by evil, but overcome evil with good.

Romans 12:21 (NKJV)

Week #34

Good Morning, today we will be reading **Proverbs 10:22** (NASB).
IT IS THE BLESSING OF THE LORD THAT MAKES RICH,
AND HE ADDS NO SORROW TO IT.

And **Proverbs 10:22** (NKJV)
THE BLESSING OF THE LORD MAKES ONE RICH,
AND HE ADDS NO SORROW WITH IT.

And **Proverbs 10:22** (HCSB)
THE LORD'S BLESSING ENRICHES,
AND STRUGGLE ADDS NOTHING TO IT.

And **Proverbs 10:22** (GW)
IT IS THE LORD'S BLESSING THAT MAKES A PERSON RICH,
AND HARD WORK ADDS NOTHING TO IT.

And again **Proverbs 10:22** (NIV)
THE BLESSING OF THE LORD BRINGS WEALTH,
WITHOUT PAINFUL TOIL FOR IT.

And finally **Proverbs 10:22** (NLT)
THE BLESSING OF THE LORD MAKES A PERSON RICH,
AND HE ADDS NO SORROW WITH IT.

The Lord our God blesses all His children. It is part of His very nature, He wants to bless, He is excited and joyful about blessing His kids. We just need to be sure that our hearts are ready to receive, then those blessings can flow. We have to know what has true, lasting, and eternal value, and what does not. We walk with Him and the blessing flows, but we do not walk with Him *so that* the blessings will flow. We seek His Face, not His Hand. And we must also always remember that people are more valuable than things. To get this backward is simply tragic. Money, wealth, and riches are for service. They are to be used as the Spirit leads us so that we may bless our brothers and sisters and further the Kingdom. Oh, what great joy to see the Hand of God arrange blessing after blessing for us. And what an even greater joy when we can take from those blessings and bless all those around us.

ALL THESE BLESSINGS WILL COME ON YOU AND ACCOMPANY YOU IF YOU OBEY THE LORD YOUR GOD: Deuteronomy 28:2 (NIV)

ALL THESE BLESSINGS WILL COME AND OVERTAKE YOU, BECAUSE YOU OBEY THE LORD YOUR GOD: Deuteronomy 28:2 (HCSB)

Walk with Him and be ready, they are coming... Talk with Him and be available for service, they are on their way...

Be excited and joyful about being able to bless someone, somehow, someway, and the blessings will overtake you...

We pray the Lord bless you, today.

A Testimony....

As I have told previously, for many years I was massively in debt, and credit card debt was a huge part of that debt. The Lord led me out and blessed me out, of all that mess I had made. Then, a few months ago, one of our banks effectively offered us $300 to start using their credit card. It caused me to reflect and thank God for all He had done. Those to whom we were once chained, were now coming to us. We no longer pay any fees or any interest (as we payoff everything each month). And now they pay us, with cash rewards, to use their cards. I was impressed yesterday to go and see what *they* owe. $1,277.68 That is what they owe, us. Isn't God good? Isn't God amazing? He can change our whole world.

When we focus on the Kingdom and others then He is free to turn everything around. He so wants to bless His kids; we just have to get our focus in the right place. **(Matthew 6:33)**

This has not been by intelligence, ability, skill, or effort. We have spent most of our years hovering at the border between low income and lower middle class. And we are still below the median household income level. This is all by His grace and by His Spirit. **(Zechariah 4:6)**

I am just a little kid from a trailer park in Oklahoma. The oil bust made an evil impression on me, but God... God healed my heart and changed my nature. He taught me to love and believe. That faith and love inspired me to give. I went and looked up the footprint of that old trailer park, now long since gone. It was about 60 acres. Now the Lord has given my family and I more than all I used to see and know. Our little farm is 80 acres, it warms my heart to see all that God has done for us. We are not exceptional, nor do we possess rare gifts and abilities. But we are His sons and daughters and we are special to Him.

As a kid, I knew the depths of poverty and as an adult, I found the tightening chains of debt, but thanks be to God that in Him there is abundance. In walking with Him, I have been delivered from poverty and freed from those chains of debt. Now, what shall we do with this deliverance, this freedom, and this abundance? Shall we hold it close and keep it for ourselves? Or, shall we seek to bless those who are where we once were? How can we ever be selfish and self-centered after seeing the breadth and width of His love and grace towards us? Shall we not endeavor by His Spirit to be as giving and generous as our Father and give our life away?

6 WHEN THE LORD YOUR GOD BLESSES YOU AS HE HAS PROMISED YOU, YOU WILL LEND TO MANY NATIONS BUT NOT BORROW; YOU WILL RULE OVER MANY NATIONS, BUT THEY WILL NOT RULE OVER YOU.
7 "IF THERE IS A POOR PERSON AMONG YOU, ONE OF YOUR BROTHERS WITHIN ANY OF YOUR GATES IN THE LAND THE LORD YOUR GOD IS GIVING YOU, YOU MUST NOT BE HARDHEARTED OR TIGHTFISTED TOWARD YOUR POOR BROTHER. 8 INSTEAD, YOU ARE TO OPEN YOUR HAND TO HIM AND FREELY LOAN HIM ENOUGH FOR WHATEVER NEED HE HAS.

Deuteronomy 15:6-8 (HCSB)

Testify...

Pray...

Prophesy...

He raises the poor
from the dust
And lifts the beggar
from the ash heap,
To set them among princes
And make them inherit the
throne of glory.
"For the pillars of the earth
are the LORD'S,
And He has set the world
upon them.

1 Samuel 2:8 (NKJV)

Week #35

Good Morning, today we will be reading **Mark 10:28-31** (NKJV).

> *²⁸ Then Peter began to say to Him, "See, we have left all and followed You."*
> *²⁹ So Jesus answered and said, "Assuredly, I say to you, there is no one who has left house or brothers or sisters or father or mother or wife or children or lands, for My sake and the gospel's, ³⁰ who shall not receive a hundredfold now in this time—houses and brothers and sisters and mothers and children and lands, with persecutions—and in the age to come, eternal life. ³¹ But many who are first will be last, and the last first."*

And **Mark 10:28-31** (NLT)

> *²⁸ Then Peter began to speak up. "We've given up everything to follow you," he said.*
> *²⁹ "Yes," Jesus replied, "and I assure you that everyone who has given up house or brothers or sisters or mother or father or children or property, for my sake and for the Good News, ³⁰ will receive now in return a hundred times as many houses, brothers, sisters, mothers, children, and property—along with persecution. And in the world to come that person will have eternal life. ³¹ But many who are the greatest now will be least important then, and those who seem least important now will be the greatest then."*

And finally, **Mark 10:28-31** (HCSB)

> *²⁸ Peter began to tell Him, "Look, we have left everything and followed You."*
> *²⁹ "I assure you," Jesus said, "there is no one who has left house, brothers or sisters, mother or father, children, or fields because of Me and the gospel, ³⁰ who will not receive 100 times more, now at this time—houses, brothers and sisters, mothers and children, and fields, with persecutions—and eternal life in the age to come. ³¹ But many who are first will be last, and the last first."*

The rich young ruler had just turned away from Jesus because he thought he had just too much to lose. He thought the price was too high. We know that following Jesus will cost us everything. We will give all we have, and all we are to Him. But that is not the end of our story... God will multiply blessings upon us exceedingly more than what we lost. 100 times or with multiples of multiples, the Lord will bless us. We then are ready to use those blessings to further the kingdom. And we know persecutions will come, but we also know that Life, *the* Eternal life, will sustain us forever.

We pray the Lord bless you, today.

A Testimony....

I began to notice a lot of my family's giving and blessings were about vehicles. So I inquired of the Lord, why, and how was this the case. He reminded me of the time just before we left for Japan that I had a youth group member who needed a vehicle. First, I loaned him my motorcycle, which was my baby. It was a tough thing for me to do, but I just wanted to help this young man. It was quite impractical to have a bike as your only vehicle, so as we prepare to leave, I made a deal with him to take/use my truck.

Well, that deal never really worked out, but I understood what it was like to start from nothing. He got the truck and it helped him get started, and that was the point. He was blessed and he did not have to worry about a vehicle, which can be a huge concern when you are just starting out in life.

It might look like we *lost* a truck, but that is not how the kingdom works. We got an absolutely perfect car for our family in Japan. It was an inexpensive, older car, but we never had any breakdowns with it in the four years we drove it. It fit us perfectly as a family, and then we were able to bless someone with it when we left Japan.

Then when we returned to the States, we were able to buy my wife her first brand new car. The Lord had blessed us so much that we didn't need financing, we were simply able to right the check (the car salespeople were not expecting that from our family's *appearance*).

Later, as I have told we bought our heroic minivan which was a blessing upon blessing to our family. Then my daughter got her perfect *for her* truck. For many years now we have had more vehicles than we can drive. God has been so gracious and abundant in his blessings, that we have a real parking problem (as problems go, it's not a bad one to have).

Leaving stuff, giving stuff for the kingdom is not the end of the story. Once our heart is right, and we have put first things first, God can begin to pour out His blessings.

GIVE, AND IT WILL BE GIVEN TO YOU. THEY WILL POUR INTO YOUR LAP A GOOD MEASURE—PRESSED DOWN, SHAKEN TOGETHER, AND RUNNING OVER. FOR BY YOUR STANDARD OF MEASURE IT WILL BE MEASURED TO YOU IN RETURN." Luke 6:38 (NASB)

Testify...

Pray...

Prophesy...

³ But You, O Lord, are a shield about me,
My glory, and the One who lifts my head.
⁴ I was crying to the Lord with my voice,
And He answered me from His holy mountain. Selah.
⁵ I lay down and slept;
I awoke, for the Lord sustains me.

Psalm 3:3-5 *(NASB)*

Week #36

Good Morning, today we will be reading **Romans 15:25-28** (NKJV).

> **²⁵ But now I am going to Jerusalem to minister to the saints. ²⁶ For it pleased those from Macedonia and Achaia to make a certain contribution for the poor among the saints who are in Jerusalem. ²⁷ It pleased them indeed, and they are their debtors. For if the Gentiles have been partakers of their spiritual things, their duty is also to minister to them in material things. ²⁸ Therefore, when I have performed this and have sealed to them this fruit, I shall go by way of you to Spain.**

And again **Romans 15:25-28** (GNT)

> **²⁵ Right now, however, I am going to Jerusalem in the service of God's people there. ²⁶ For the churches in Macedonia and Achaia have freely decided to give an offering to help the poor among God's people in Jerusalem. ²⁷ That decision was their own; but, as a matter of fact, they have an obligation to help them. Since the Jews shared their spiritual blessings with the Gentiles, the Gentiles ought to use their material blessings to help the Jews. ²⁸ When I have finished this task and have turned over to them all the money that has been raised for them, I shall leave for Spain and visit you on my way there.**

And finally, **Romans 15:25-28** (NLT)

> **²⁵ But before I come, I must go to Jerusalem to take a gift to the believers there. ²⁶ For you see, the believers in Macedonia and Achaia have eagerly taken up an offering for the poor among the believers in Jerusalem. ²⁷ They were glad to do this because they feel they owe a real debt to them. Since the Gentiles received the spiritual blessings of the Good News from the believers in Jerusalem, they feel the least they can do in return is to help them financially. ²⁸ As soon as I have delivered this money and completed this good deed of theirs, I will come to see you on my way to Spain.**

I hope we see those keywords. *Gift...* It is a gift even to those we *owe... Eagerly*, give the gift and be *pleased* to do so... *Glad* to do this... We do owe a debt to those that help us spiritually... But we repay that debt not out of compulsion or in drudgery, but we eagerly and gladly give our gifts to help them financially, this is merely the beginning of what we can do for them.

We pray the Lord bless you, today.

A Testimony....

I have a good friend who invited me out to eat one evening. I had been able to bless this friend in several small ways over the years. So, he adamantly insisted on paying for the meal. I did protest but he was right, and I had to relent. Isn't this how the children of God should be? Desiring to bless each other, debating who *gets to* bless and who *has to* receive the blessing. Don't get me wrong, it is a great honor to be blessed by a child of God, and we should receive those things gladly. But if we have our preference, shouldn't we want to be the giver?

'IT IS MORE BLESSED TO GIVE THAN TO RECEIVE.'
Acts 20:35b (NASB)

A few weeks later four of us friends from church were meeting at a restaurant to celebrate a birthday. I just so happened to get there first and arranged to pay for the meal. My good friend did call me to say that he wanted to pay for the meal. But I was able to point out that he paid for our last meal. He did protest but, in the end, he had to relent. My spirit was leaping for joy merely at this debate between us. Both of us wanted to be the ones to bless this group. Both of us wanted to be a blessing much more than we wanted to receive a blessing.

That meal was wonderful and I don't really mean the food. We talked about the goodness of God. We shared stories of the grace of God. We told testimonies of the hand of God on our lives. We were not endeavoring to be loud, nor were we cowering in the corner. Later we had a couple came up to our table and said they loved hearing us tell of the goodness of God. They also shared with us how God had blessed them with their own business and how His hand was making it a success. We only broke up the meal because we could see it was getting late, so out of respect for the restaurant staff, we called it a night.

God's way is always best. That was somewhere in the top three social events of my life. This new nature He gives us does not deprive us of life, it unleashes life (**John 10:10**). My old nature would have always been counting the cost of that meal. It would have been considering whether it was a good deal. It would have wondered why didn't the wealthiest guy pay. It would have tracked if the guys were thankful *enough*. Yuck... Thank you, Father, for this new heart you have given to us (**2 Corinthians 5:17**). It is such a joy, to consider others more than ourselves and value people far more than money.

Testify...

Pray...

Prophesy...

[But what of that?] For I consider that the sufferings of this present time (this present life) are not worth being compared with the glory that is about to be revealed to us and in us and for us and conferred on us!

Romans 8:18 (AMPC)

Week #37

Good Morning, today we will be reading **2 Corinthians 8:1-4** (GNT).

¹ Our friends, we want you to know what God's grace has accomplished in the churches in Macedonia. ² They have been severely tested by the troubles they went through; but their joy was so great that they were extremely generous in their giving, even though they are very poor. ³ I can assure you that they gave as much as they could, and even more than they could. Of their own free will ⁴ they begged us and pleaded for the privilege of having a part in helping God's people in Judea.

And **2 Corinthians 8:1-4** (NASB)

¹ Now, brethren, we wish to make known to you the grace of God which has been given in the churches of Macedonia, ² that in a great ordeal of affliction their abundance of joy and their deep poverty overflowed in the wealth of their liberality. ³ For I testify that according to their ability, and beyond their ability, they gave of their own accord, ⁴ begging us with much urging for the favor of participation in the support of the saints,

And again **2 Corinthians 8:1-4** (HCSB)

¹ We want you to know, brothers, about the grace of God granted to the churches of Macedonia: ² During a severe testing by affliction, their abundance of joy and their deep poverty overflowed into the wealth of their generosity. ³ I testify that, on their own, according to their ability and beyond their ability, ⁴ they begged us insistently for the privilege of sharing in the ministry to the saints,

And finally, **2 Corinthians 8:1-4** (NLT)

¹ Now I want you to know, dear brothers and sisters, what God in his kindness has done through the churches in Macedonia. ² They are being tested by many troubles, and they are very poor. But they are also filled with abundant joy, which has overflowed in rich generosity. ³ For I can testify that they gave not only what they could afford, but far more. And they did it of their own free will. ⁴ They begged us again and again for the privilege of sharing in the gift for the believers in Jerusalem.

Look what a heart for God's Kingdom will do. Look what true love for our brothers and sisters will do. Even those who are "very poor" were filled with abundant joy and gave generously. Of their own free will they gave, they begged again and again to have the privilege of giving to the believers, to bless the Kingdom of God.

Then verse 5 goes on to tell us that they gave beyond what Paul had expected, or hoped for.

We pray the Lord bless you, today.

A Testimony....

One late spring day, my neighbor set a huge amount of junk out on the curb for the trash men to take away. In the pile of stuff was an old snowblower. When I saw it, my spirit urged me to go get it, but my brain struggled to understand why. I am originally from Oklahoma where snow is rare and fleeting. So while we lived up north, I wanted to enjoy the snow. Even shoveling was, to me, part of the experience, so I never bought a snowblower. But my spirit just would not let me rest. Maybe I could use the motor and parts for something on the farm? I walked over and saved the little machine from its destination, the landfill.

Then over the next several days, it seemed like every time I needed something in my garage that snowblower was in the way. I moved it from here to there and back again. I got so frustrated that I decided to set it back out for the trash men to pick up.

A few days later, I was talking with a friend of mine and he was telling me of a blessing of the Lord. We had just come out of a very long, cold, and snowing winter. He has a very long driveway. It runs from the street all the way down along the side of his house to his garage at the back of his property. So, he has 3-4 times as much to shovel as I do. He had asked the Lord to provide a snowblower for his family. He told me that he had found a used, but nice, machine for sale. But as he made arrangements to buy and pick up this machine, the lady selling it just gave it to him. She also gave him another smaller snowblower that wasn't working.

He was rejoicing that the Lord had doubly blessed him. He was planning on repairing the smaller machine, so he and his son could both clear snow at the same time. We were talking over his ideas of what it needed. I began to tell him about this little snowblower, I had. I told him my story, still confused about what to do with it. I offered to give it to him for parts, but parts don't just crossover from different brands and models. He described what he had and it sounded similar to the one I had. Then we checked, we each had the same brand and model. It quickly and finally all made sense to my brain, this machine was for him. I was so happy to receive understanding and get it out of my garage.

My friend got the one I had, running with no problem. He then got his little one running with only minor repairs. So now he had three snowblowers. He was able to bless someone else who was in need and still have a double blessing for his family.

Testify...

Pray...

Prophesy...

All these blessings will come upon you and overtake you if you obey the Lord your God:

Deuteronomy 28:2 (NASB)

Week #38

Good Morning, today we will be reading 2 Corinthians 8:6-9 (NKJV).

⁶ So we urged Titus, that as he had begun, so he would also complete this grace in you as well. ⁷ But as you abound in everything—in faith, in speech, in knowledge, in all diligence, and in your love for us—see that you abound in this grace also.

⁸ I speak not by commandment, but I am testing the sincerity of your love by the diligence of others. ⁹ For you know the grace of our Lord Jesus Christ, that though He was rich, yet for your sakes He became poor, that you through His poverty might become rich.

And again 2 Corinthians 8:6-9 (GNT)

⁶ So we urged Titus, who began this work, to continue it and help you complete this special service of love. ⁷ You are so rich in all you have: in faith, speech, and knowledge, in your eagerness to help and in your love for us. And so we want you to be generous also in this service of love.

⁸ I am not laying down any rules. But by showing how eager others are to help, I am trying to find out how real your own love is. ⁹ You know the grace of our Lord Jesus Christ; rich as he was, he made himself poor for your sake, in order to make you rich by means of his poverty.

And finally, 2 Corinthians 8:6-9 (NLT)

⁶ So we have urged Titus, who encouraged your giving in the first place, to return to you and encourage you to finish this ministry of giving. ⁷ Since you excel in so many ways—in your faith, your gifted speakers, your knowledge, your enthusiasm, and your love from us—I want you to excel also in this gracious act of giving.

⁸ I am not commanding you to do this. But I am testing how genuine your love is by comparing it with the eagerness of the other churches.

⁹ You know the generous grace of our Lord Jesus Christ. Though he was rich, yet for your sakes he became poor, so that by his poverty he could make you rich.

2 Corinthians chapter 8 is clearly speaking of financial giving, with translations using chapter headings like:

A Call to Generous Giving - Great Generosity
Christian Giving - And Excel in Giving.

Paul wants the Church at Corinth to excel in giving the same way they excel in many other ways like faith, knowledge, and love. He does not give them a command or layout a set of rules to follow, but calls on them to be led and inspired by love.

We pray the Lord bless you, today.

A Testimony....

I have told of the fearfulness, faithless, selfishness of my heart before the Lord gave me a new heart. What is amazing to me is that there were almost two decades between my developing faith in God to heal my body and my developing faith in God to bless and keep me financially. This illustrates just how bad that old heart was, but it also shows me the patience and kindness of my Father. He still walked with me, He still let me develop where I could. He knew that change would come, and He did not throw me away out of frustration or impatience.

I often see a staircase out in front of me, with so many steps that it gets pretty daunting. But then I turn and see a great many steps that God has already brought me up. These both give me great inspiration and hope. We all have a long way to go, but He has already brought us so very far. He will not fail in helping us up each and every step.

With all this said, there are still many times that the Lord will bring before me something more in my heart that needs changing. I remember attending one lovely church, that had a great pastor and wonderful people. But their doctrine on money and giving to the kingdom, it just didn't seem right, to me. So, I withheld most of my giving. I had a doctrinal reason; I didn't want to be a part of that teaching. I didn't want to join in and support or promote that teaching. But doctrine, reason, and principals should never separate us from our brothers and sisters. If we are waiting for everyone to be perfect before we join in the walk and the kingdom, we will be on the sidelines for a long, long time.

(*Of course, I'm not talking about supporting something truly blasphemous or evil.*)

The Lord continued to work on my heart. Years later in a new city and a new church, I heard the pastor's microphone was out. They needed to buy a new one. I had not been going to this church for very long, and I was not familiar with their denomination at all. So, my doctrine again tried to rise up and say there was no way we could buy that mic. We're just not sure what would be said through it, so how could we be a part of that? But Love... I knew this pastor's heart, he loves God and he just wants to help the people. I am very sure that I will not agree with every single word that passes through that mic, but still, I want to help this man, this church, and the kingdom. He is my brother; I will not wait for his perfection to walk alongside him. Would I want God to do the same to me? Lord forgive me for all those evil judgments I have leveled over the years.

The microphone turned out to cost more than $800, and my brain began to seize up, but money seems so worthless when love is present. Was not my brother worth this? Was not my pastor, and the church worth this? Wasn't preaching, teaching, and helping people worth this? That $800 just fades to nothing and joy, excitement, and purpose shines bright.

Testify...

Pray...

Prophesy...

¹⁸ "Come now, and let us reason together,"
Says the LORD,
"Though your sins are as scarlet,
They will be as white as snow;
Though they are red like crimson,
They will be like wool.
¹⁹ "If you consent and obey,
You will eat
the best of the land;

Isaiah 1:18-19 (NASB)

Week #39

Good Morning, today we will be reading **2 Corinthians 8:10-12** (NLT).
¹⁰ Here is my advice: It would be good for you to finish what you started a year ago. Last year you were the first who wanted to give, and you were the first to begin doing it. ¹¹ Now you should finish what you started. Let the eagerness you showed in the beginning be matched now by your giving. Give in proportion to what you have. ¹² Whatever you give is acceptable if you give it eagerly. And give according to what you have, not what you don't have.

And again **2 Corinthians 8:10-12** (NKJV)
¹⁰ And in this I give advice: It is to your advantage not only to be doing what you began and were desiring to do a year ago; ¹¹ but now you also must complete the doing of it; that as there was a readiness to desire it, so there also may be a completion out of what you have. ¹² For if there is first a willing mind, it is accepted according to what one has, and not according to what he does not have.

And finally, **2 Corinthians 8:10-12** (NASB)
¹⁰ I give my opinion in this matter, for this is to your advantage, who were the first to begin a year ago not only to do this, but also to desire to do it. ¹¹ But now finish doing it also, so that just as there was the readiness to desire it, so there may be also the completion of it by your ability. ¹² For if the readiness is present, it is acceptable according to what a person has, not according to what he does not have.

We are not forced, compelled, threatened, or coerced to give. We are led by the Spirit and He will always show us what we should do in all things including financial matters. When He leads us to give and we willingly and joyfully choose to obey that leading, then we should also be faithful in that matter. Anxious thoughts may attempt to pressure us, but we remain faithful. Even apathy and slothfulness can creep in but we should always remain faithful with the gracious help of His Spirit. Out of what we have right before us, we can show our love for our God, His Kingdom, and our brothers and sisters. Thanks be to God it is not some set amount, that some could never reach while others could attain it easily. We can give simply and peaceably out of what we do have. And when we give willingly, joyfully, and faithfully, our gifts will be acceptable to our Father. When we give out of a heart of love the willingness, joyfulness, and the faithfulness will always be there.

We pray the Lord bless you, today.

A Testimony....

For years I have worked and struggled to get everything set up on our farm for when we retire. I have spent hundreds of hours at auctions and thousands of hours in online auctions trying to get the perfect piece of equipment for just the right price. None of it actually ever works out unless I turn it over to God and let myself be led by His Spirit.

One of the areas of concern about equipment for me is mowing. We mow about 5-6 acres. It usually takes us about 8 hours to mow, and that is with my daughter on a riding mower, my son on a ZTR mower, and me on a tractor pulling a brush hog. Well last summer, the riding mower became in need of real repairs. So, I began searching for another piece of equipment. I had always wanted to try a finish mower to use with my tractor, but I didn't know how well they would work. And besides, the good ones were over $2,000. I found several on auctions, but nothing ever worked out.

Well, the next summer came around and I still didn't have that riding mower fixed or anything to replace it. This normally would have sent me into a working frenzy; searching, researching, and planning for hours each day. But the Lord stilled my heart and helped me focus on doing those things that He has called me to do.

Then with next to no effort at all on my part, there was a finish mower. It was bought by a farmer but it was actually never used. I bid and watched the auction but not with the intensity that I normally do. I was able, by the grace of God and His Spirit, to keep that on the back burner and focus on the much more important Kingdom work. It was valued at well over $2,000, and I had set aside $1,500 to buy it. But God... I got the mower with a bid of $400. That's not even the real testimony.

Pulling my brush hog behind my tractor is such slow, monotonous work that it can be very mentally taxing for me. We hooked this new mower up to a nice tractor (one of the ones God provided when I challenged him, Week#12). This set up of His equipment is faster than everything else we have. It has such a good cut that you can't tell the difference between it and the ZTR. The last time we mowed, when we were all done for the day, I went to take this tractor and finish mower back to the barn. Then I decided I would mow a little extra around a pond and an old goat pen. And I just kept doing more and more, and I noticed I was smiling and having fun. Then it hit me, the most arduous chore I had to do on the farm, God just made it enjoyable. His tractor and His mower were a perfect combo to do the job, to do it quickly, to do it well, and to make it enjoyable to me. Now, I know that slinging a finish mower around behind a tractor for hours and hours might not be your bliss, but it is mine. I love hearing His tractor run, I love mowing His property quickly, efficiently, and doing it well. He wants to walk us right into our joy. He wants our life and our work meaningful and joyful. We just have to trust and obey, and just let Him lead.

Testify...

Pray...

Prophesy...

⁵ Trust in the LORD with all your heart, And lean not on your own understanding; ⁶ In all your ways acknowledge Him, And He shall direct your paths.

Proverbs 3:5-6 (NKJV)

Week #40

Good Morning, today we will be reading **2 Corinthians 8:13-15** (NLT).

¹³ Of course, I don't mean your giving should make life easy for others and hard for yourselves. I only mean that there should be some equality. ¹⁴ Right now you have plenty and can help those who are in need. Later, they will have plenty and can share with you when you need it. In this way, things will be equal. ¹⁵ As the Scriptures say, "Those who gathered a lot had nothing left over, and those who gathered only a little had enough."

And **2 Corinthians 8:13-15** (NASB)

¹³ For this is not for the ease of others and for your affliction, but by way of equality— ¹⁴ at this present time your abundance being a supply for their need, so that their abundance also may become a supply for your need, that there may be equality; ¹⁵ as it is written, "He who gathered much did not have too much, and he who gathered little had no lack."

And let's read **2 Corinthians 9:1-2** (NASB)

¹ For it is superfluous for me to write to you about this ministry to the saints; ² for I know your readiness, of which I boast about you to the Macedonians, namely, that Achaia has been prepared since last year, and your zeal has stirred up most of them.

And again **2 Corinthians 9:1-2** (NKJV)

¹ Now concerning the ministering to the saints, it is superfluous for me to write to you; ² for I know your willingness, about which I boast of you to the Macedonians, that Achaia was ready a year ago; and your zeal has stirred up the majority.

And finally, **2 Corinthians 9:1-2** (GNT)

¹ There is really no need for me to write you about the help being sent to God's people in Judea. ² I know that you are willing to help, and I have boasted of you to the people in Macedonia. "The believers in Achaia," I said, "have been ready to help since last year." Your eagerness has stirred up most of them.

We are the Body of Christ and members in particular. So there should be a willingness to help our brother and sisters who are in need. We cannot simply leave them behind, and we could never truly abound in blessing while they suffer in need. So let our eagerness and zeal to help them, abound. This heart of love and compassion will inspire many others to engage in giving and helping our dear brothers and sisters in the Lord.

We pray the Lord bless you, today.

A Testimony....

I have a good friend that I used to run with, for mile after mile we would discuss all the topics of life. Our families were like mirror images of each other. He worked and his wife stayed home with their two small boys, and my wife worked while I stayed home with my young son and daughter. We attended the same church but we came from very different backgrounds. He came from a very traditional denominational upbringing. Generally speaking, he relegated the spiritual things of this life to God, but the everyday natural things were up to us. It seemed quite odd to him when I would tell of God working in my everyday life. It seemed even more strange to him that God would get involved in such a lowly thing as money.

He would always let me tell my stories. But I knew he just could not see how Almighty God would have anything to do with such mundane and terrestrial things. In a sense, he was right that these things are so far beneath our God, that He should never get His Hands dirty with such matters. But He simply loves us that much. He loves us enough to stoop down and help us with all these silly natural, earthly matters that we deem so important. He doesn't stand on high and command us to be better than all this **(John 2:1-10)**. He comes to help. Just look at our Jesus, He became one of us and He knows our walk in this world **(Hebrews 4:15)**.

I never tried to push my friend into my way of walking with God, I just told the stories of my everyday walk with God. After a few years of our training together, He told me that he and his wife had decided to begin to trust God to get them out of debt. He had seen the difference between our families. Our families' incomes were almost identical, our situations and lifestyles were also nearly identical. But his family was treading water financially. They had loan payments and credit card payments that only let them live from one paycheck to the next. My family was free of debt, we were free to give and free to live **(Proverbs 22:7)**. This was not because we were smarter or better with money. This was not because we were better Christians or because God loved us more. The only difference between our families was that we had opened the door to our finances and invited God in. We had invited Him to lead, to guide, to bless, and to keep us in the financial arena.

Soon after this, our two families moved to different cities. But within a year, I got a call from my friend. He was rejoicing as he told that his family was now completely out of debt, to the glory of God. And before the next year was up, He called again. They had bought a house in their home town and were remodeling it to use it for a rental property. Everything had changed for them, simply because they invited God into that part of their life. His blessing freed them from debt and brought them to a place of more than enough.

Testify...

Pray...

Prophesy...

¹ Therefore, since we have so great a cloud of witnesses surrounding us, let us also lay aside every encumbrance and the sin which so easily entangles us, and let us run with endurance the race that is set before us, ² fixing our eyes on Jesus, the author and perfecter of faith, who for the joy set before Him endured the cross, despising the shame, and has sat down at the right hand of the throne of God.

Hebrews 12:1-2 (NASB)

Week #41

Good Morning, today we will be reading **2 Corinthians 9:5-9** (GNT).

⁵ So I thought it was necessary to urge these believers to go to you ahead of me and get ready in advance the gift you promised to make. Then it will be ready when I arrive, and it will show that you give because you want to, not because you have to.
⁶ Remember that the person who plants few seeds will have a small crop; the one who plants many seeds will have a large crop. ⁷ You should each give, then, as you have decided, not with regret or out of a sense of duty; for God loves the one who gives gladly. ⁸ And God is able to give you more than you need, so that you will always have all you need for yourselves and more than enough for every good cause. ⁹ As the scripture says,
"He gives generously to the needy;
His kindness lasts forever."

And 2 Corinthians 9:5-9 (NASB)

⁵ So I thought it necessary to urge the brethren that they would go on ahead to you and arrange beforehand your previously promised bountiful gift, so that the same would be ready as a bountiful gift and not affected by covetousness.
⁶ Now this I say, he who sows sparingly will also reap sparingly, and he who sows bountifully will also reap bountifully. ⁷ Each one must do just as he has purposed in his heart, not grudgingly or under compulsion, for God loves a cheerful giver. ⁸ And God is able to make all grace abound to you, so that always having all sufficiency in everything, you may have an abundance for every good deed; ⁹ as it is written,
"He scattered abroad, he gave to the poor,
His righteousness endures forever."

And finally, 2 Corinthians 9:5-9 (NLT)

⁵ So I thought I should send these brothers ahead of me to make sure the gift you promised is ready. But I want it to be a willing gift, not one given grudgingly.
⁶ Remember this—a farmer who plants only a few seeds will get a small crop. But the one who plants generously will get a generous crop. ⁷ You must each decide in your heart how much to give. And don't give reluctantly or in response to pressure. "For God loves a person who gives cheerfully." ⁸ And God will generously provide all you need. Then you will always have everything you need and plenty left over to share with others.
⁹ As the Scriptures say,
"They share freely and give generously to the poor.
Their good deeds will be remembered forever."

We should always do as we have promised, and in giving especially, we should keep our heart willing and joyful. We should also know that giving has a return. It is a spiritual law. Giving cheerfully that which you have decided to give will never lead to your lack but rather to abundance. The harvest will be beyond your need over into abundance. And what shall we do with that abundance? Will not our willing, cheerful heart lead us to once again plant a generous crop?

We pray the Lord bless you, today.

A Testimony....

One day after a bible study, I was looking over some books they had, when I overheard a conversation. A man had ordered a book and it had come in early. It was so early that the man had not expected it and didn't bring any money to pay for the book. It was a small amount and no real concern; he would simply bring the money next week.

I stepped over to him and apologized for intruding and overhearing, but I asked if he would let me pay for the book. He really seemed perplexed. First, he thought I meant to pay for it, and then he could pay me back. But when I asked if I could simply pay for it just to be a blessing, he seemed even more confused. He even seemed a little insulted. As a man and one brought up in rural America, I understood. *Ego and the whole bootstraps thing are real in this part of the world.* It was like I was implying that he *needed* my help. He tried to explain that money was not an issue at all. With a few words, I reassured him that I understood. I just simply wanted to bless a brother in the Lord with a book. Hoping that book would be a blessing to him and help him in his walk with the Lord. Then I could see all that confusion and ego fade away. He gladly received that book and thanked me for blessing him.

Sometimes for some of us, receiving is a difficult thing to handle.

Some weeks later over by those same books, I saw this same man buy a book for someone else. He had noticed another man looking at a book that he had already read. He asked him if he could buy that book for him. He told the man that he knew it to be a good book and he was sure it would bless him. He then had to face a similar reaction as to his own. The other man explained he had the money; he didn't *need* someone to buy the book for him. But he persisted with a little explanation and showing a heart that just wanted to bless.

It was a nice thing to bless my brother with a book, but what a better thing it was to open up a world of being a blessing. I know our culture of independence and self-reliance is deeply engrained in us. But we are in our Father's Kingdom now. We are one body now. We need each other, and we want to help and bless each other.

FROM WHOM THE WHOLE BODY, BEING FITTED AND HELD TOGETHER BY WHAT EVERY JOINT SUPPLIES, ACCORDING TO THE PROPER WORKING OF EACH INDIVIDUAL PART, CAUSES THE GROWTH OF THE BODY FOR THE BUILDING UP OF ITSELF IN LOVE.

Ephesians 4:16 (NASB)

Testify...

Pray...

Prophesy...

The LORD is my shepherd, I shall not want.

Psalms 23:1 (NASB)

Week #42

Good Morning, today we will be reading 2 Corinthians 9:10-15 (NLT).
10 For God is the one who provides seed for the farmer and then bread to eat. In the same way, he will provide and increase your resources and then produce a great harvest of generosity in you.
11 Yes, you will be enriched in every way so that you can always be generous. And when we take your gifts to those who need them, they will thank God. 12 So two good things will result from this ministry of giving—the needs of the believers in Jerusalem will be met, and they will joyfully express their thanks to God.
13 As a result of your ministry, they will give glory to God. For your generosity to them and to all believers will prove that you are obedient to the Good News of Christ. 14 And they will pray for you with deep affection because of the overflowing grace God has given to you. 15 Thank God for this gift too wonderful for words!

And 2 Corinthians 9:10-15 (NKJV)
10 Now may He who supplies seed to the sower, and bread for food, supply and multiply the seed you have *sown* and increase the fruits of your righteousness, 11 while *you are* enriched in everything for all liberality, which causes thanksgiving through us to God. 12 For the administration of this service not only supplies the needs of the saints, but also is abounding through many thanksgivings to God, 13 while, through the proof of this ministry, they glorify God for the obedience of your confession to the gospel of Christ, and for *your* liberal sharing with them and all *men*, 14 and by their prayer for you, who long for you because of the exceeding grace of God in you. 15 Thanks *be* to God for His indescribable gift!

The indescribable gift, too wonderful for words.... The gift of allowing us to participate in the kingdom through giving. The gift of making a way for us to bless our brothers and sisters in the Lord and show our love for them through our giving. God could do this all without us. God really supplies it all anyway. But He has allowed the gift of blessings to flow through us. So that we may express our love one for another. So that we may show how precious the people and the kingdom are to us. He blesses us and then we can choose to try and keep those blessings, all to ourselves, or we can choose to give. We can choose to give our life away through our giving, then we can begin to look and act like our precious Savior who gave all for us.

We pray the Lord bless you, today.

A Testimony....

One of our neighbors knew that I scouted and attended a lot of auctions, so they asked me if I ever came across any treadmills. I told them what I had seen quality and pricing wise.

As we talked, I was considering whether to offer them our treadmill that was just sitting in storage down at the farm. My brain didn't want to bring it up because I thought it was just not good enough. It was more of *a go for a walk* treadmill, instead of *a go for a real brisk run* treadmill. But the Spirit kept bringing it up, so I offered it to them.

They, of course, resisted the gift at first and offered to pay for it. They were a young couple with a new child just getting started in life, so I had to insist it be a gift. I told them it was a basic treadmill and it would be weeks or months before I could bring it up from the farm. I soon persuaded them to let me bless them with this gift, which I personally didn't feel was that great a gift at all.

Well, eventually we got the treadmill brought up from the farm and checked it all out. It did have much better function than form, so I brought them over to check it out. I wondered if they might just pass it up and look for something better. But they received it with joy and thankfulness. I really did not consider this much of a blessing or gift. I didn't see this as some great arrangement of God or some great leading by His Spirit.

Well over a year later, in a normal little talk with these same neighbors. We began to talk about running, exercise, and health, etc... They again thanked us for the treadmill and told us about some health issues they had. These would not have been expected based on their age and demeanor. It then hit me that the small, insignificant, and not really good enough gift, was in fact a big deal. We were overjoyed that we could help and be a blessing.

To see the hand of God taking care of His children is always an amazing thing. I bought that treadmill at a garage sale in North Dakota. I only went to that sale to help a friend if he needed help loading up the things he wanted to buy. We never used the treadmill and then sent it down to the farm in Oklahoma when we moved. Then it was brought back up to Nebraska to be a gift. It took about 3 years and 1,500 miles to get to where it was needed. I didn't know its purpose, but God did. He certainly has plans to watch over and care for each and every one of us (**Jeremiah 29:11**).

Testify...

_____
_____
_____
_____
_____
_____

Pray...

_____
_____
_____
_____
_____
_____

Prophesy...

_____
_____
_____
_____
_____

9 But you are
A CHOSEN RACE,
A royal PRIESTHOOD,
A HOLY NATION,
A PEOPLE FOR God's
OWN POSSESSION,
so that you may proclaim the excellencies of Him who has called you out of darkness into His marvelous light;
10 for you once were NOT A PEOPLE, but now you are THE PEOPLE OF GOD;
you had NOT RECEIVED MERCY, but now you have RECEIVED MERCY.

1 Peter 2:9-10 (NASB)

Week #43

Good Morning, today we will be reading **1 John 4:11-12** (GNT).
DEAR FRIENDS, IF THIS IS HOW GOD LOVED US, THEN WE SHOULD LOVE ONE ANOTHER. NO ONE HAS EVER SEEN GOD, BUT IF WE LOVE ONE ANOTHER, GOD LIVES IN UNION WITH US, AND HIS LOVE IS MADE PERFECT IN US.

When God revealed His love for us in the sending of His Son Jesus to become one of us and then to die for us, it inspired us to love. We love Him and because we love Him, we love what He loves. We love others because they are the beloved of our beloved.

And **Mark 8:35** (NKJV)
FOR WHOEVER DESIRES TO SAVE HIS LIFE WILL LOSE IT, BUT WHOEVER LOSES HIS LIFE FOR MY SAKE AND THE GOSPEL'S WILL SAVE IT.

Our life has been secured in the sacrifice of Jesus. We no longer have to fight and struggle to find and hold life. Now we can rest in Jesus and be free to give of ourselves, for others. Love inspires us to do as was done for us. To actively give our life away. It is in these love-inspired actions that we find true life.

Remember **Luke 6:38** (NKJV)
GIVE, AND IT WILL BE GIVEN TO YOU: GOOD MEASURE, PRESSED DOWN, SHAKEN TOGETHER, AND RUNNING OVER WILL BE PUT INTO YOUR BOSOM. FOR WITH THE SAME MEASURE THAT YOU USE, IT WILL BE MEASURED BACK TO YOU."

When we trade our time, our effort, our knowledge, and our skill to others in exchange for compensation, money, then that money is a representation of a part of our life. It is also a means to procure and secure things necessary for our life. When we can give parts and pieces of that away, then we are truly giving away our life. Money in and of itself is of little value, but when you can use it to give away your life then it can mean something. When we can use it to help others and show them the love of God, then it can attain real value. Then, we are acting like our Big Brother, Jesus. And following the example of Love, Himself.

Finally, let's read **1 John 4:11-12** (NLT)
[11] DEAR FRIENDS, SINCE GOD LOVED US THAT MUCH, WE SURELY OUGHT TO LOVE EACH OTHER. [12] NO ONE HAS EVER SEEN GOD. BUT IF WE LOVE EACH OTHER, GOD LIVES IN US, AND HIS LOVE IS BROUGHT TO FULL EXPRESSION IN US.

We pray the Lord bless you, today.

A Testimony....

Just this last week a little neighbor girl came to our door and asked if she could mow our lawn for $15. My daughter had answered the door and came upstairs nearly pleading for me to let the little girl mow. My brain could barely compute all this.

This was at our home in Nebraska, which is a subdivision home with a small yard. I have a 17-year-old daughter and a 14-year-old son. I don't really need a little girl to come and mow my lawn.

We have a push mower that we have used to mow our lawn for years. Recently I bought a ZTR for the farm, but we haven't sent it to the farm, yet. So, I have a giant (considering our lawn) mower that we have used for the last several weeks. We have been mowing our yard in like 15 minutes with the ZTR. Why would I need a little girl to mow our yard?

This ZTR is so quick and easy that we volunteered to mow the yard of our neighbor for free. So why would I pay someone else to mow my own lawn?

Can you see my dilemma? But my daughter was so excited to help this little girl in her endeavor. She even offered to pay the little girl herself, and $15 was all the money my daughter had. I just couldn't say no, but I couldn't bring myself to say yes either. So, I punted. I told my daughter to tell the little girl to come back on Saturday and she could mow the lawn.

It was only a couple of days till that Saturday, but they were not easy ones for me. I knew I had done wrong; I knew I should have been more spontaneously generous. I should not have made that little girl wait. I was really hoping that she would return on Saturday, for my own sake. Now, my brain still could not reconcile the facts of the situation with what I knew was the right thing to do, but what is right, is right.

Thanks be to God, the little girl showed up on Saturday and mowed the lawn. My daughter watched over her and paid her the $15 out of her own pocket. Then this morning I looked out at the back yard and it made me smile. That yard had high and low patches, stripes, strips, and some mohawks. But it was a good thing to do. An illogical, unreasonable, and financially irresponsible; good thing to do. I just hope to hear better and respond quicker the next time God lays an opportunity to be generous before me. We are His children, we should be those "peculiar" people that are led by His Spirit.

Testify...

Pray...

Prophesy...

⁴ But God, who is rich in mercy, because of His great love with which He loved us, ⁵ even when we were dead in trespasses, made us alive together with Christ (by grace you have been saved), ⁶ and raised us up together, and made us sit together in the heavenly places in Christ Jesus, ⁷ that in the ages to come He might show the exceeding riches of His grace in His kindness toward us in Christ Jesus.

Ephesians 2:4-7 *(NKJV)*

Week #44

Good Morning, today we will be reading **James 5:1-6** (NASB).

COME NOW, YOU RICH, WEEP AND HOWL FOR YOUR MISERIES WHICH ARE COMING UPON YOU. 2 YOUR RICHES HAVE ROTTED AND YOUR GARMENTS HAVE BECOME MOTH-EATEN. 3 YOUR GOLD AND YOUR SILVER HAVE RUSTED; AND THEIR RUST WILL BE A WITNESS AGAINST YOU AND WILL CONSUME YOUR FLESH LIKE FIRE. IT IS IN THE LAST DAYS THAT YOU HAVE STORED UP YOUR TREASURE! 4 BEHOLD, THE PAY OF THE LABORERS WHO MOWED YOUR FIELDS, AND WHICH HAS BEEN WITHHELD BY YOU, CRIES OUT AGAINST YOU; AND THE OUTCRY OF THOSE WHO DID THE HARVESTING HAS REACHED THE EARS OF THE LORD OF SABAOTH. 5 YOU HAVE LIVED LUXURIOUSLY ON THE EARTH AND LED A LIFE OF WANTON PLEASURE; YOU HAVE FATTENED YOUR HEARTS IN A DAY OF SLAUGHTER. 6 YOU HAVE CONDEMNED AND PUT TO DEATH THE RIGHTEOUS MAN; HE DOES NOT RESIST YOU.

And **James 5:1-6** (NLT)

LOOK HERE, YOU RICH PEOPLE: WEEP AND GROAN WITH ANGUISH BECAUSE OF ALL THE TERRIBLE TROUBLES AHEAD OF YOU. 2 YOUR WEALTH IS ROTTING AWAY, AND YOUR FINE CLOTHES ARE MOTH-EATEN RAGS. 3 YOUR GOLD AND SILVER ARE CORRODED. THE VERY WEALTH YOU WERE COUNTING ON WILL EAT AWAY YOUR FLESH LIKE FIRE. THIS CORRODED TREASURE YOU HAVE HOARDED WILL TESTIFY AGAINST YOU ON THE DAY OF JUDGMENT. 4 FOR LISTEN! HEAR THE CRIES OF THE FIELD WORKERS WHOM YOU HAVE CHEATED OF THEIR PAY. THE CRIES OF THOSE WHO HARVEST YOUR FIELDS HAVE REACHED THE EARS OF THE LORD OF HEAVEN'S ARMIES.
5 YOU HAVE SPENT YOUR YEARS ON EARTH IN LUXURY, SATISFYING YOUR EVERY DESIRE. YOU HAVE FATTENED YOURSELVES FOR THE DAY OF SLAUGHTER. 6 YOU HAVE CONDEMNED AND KILLED INNOCENT PEOPLE, WHO DO NOT RESIST YOU.

We never want to dismiss or edit out anything in God's Word. We *do* want to take it, receive it, study it, and let it teach us all it has to give. Here we see a harsh rebuke against the rich. These rich have trusted and counted on their wealth to save and provide for them; don't do that. These rich have cheated their workers; don't do that. These rich have left their harvesters to starve; don't do that. They only think of themselves, and they even condemn and kill the righteous; really, really, don't do that.

Let our wealth, abundance, riches (to whatever degree we may attain) be a blessing to all those around us. Let our life and our money not be about us, but about others. Then... **Matthew 6:19-21**

We pray the Lord bless you, today.

A Testimony....

This is a strange testimony. I have often given away things or helped people out and later found out they were "better off" than me. Let me just give this one example. There was a man at church one day and he was telling about some difficulty he was having moving some things around on his property. I happened to have a 3-point load carrier for a tractor and offered to give it to him.

Of course, he said I didn't need to do that. But I explained I had bought it at auction for truly next to nothing and I had never used it. So, he agreed to let me bless him with it and we set a day and time for me to bring it to him.

I had never been to his home, but I knew from our talks at church he had 80 acres like we did. When I got to his home, he and his wife were so nice. They thanked us and even brought us into their home for ice cream, the real home-made stuff. He really had a nice house, way nicer than mine. He also had a practically brand-new tractor and a shop building that could swallow my house whole.

Over the next few days this began to really grate on me. I had a hard time letting this go. He had a nicer everything than I did, why was I giving things to him? Now, I had paid almost nothing for that carrier, and I volunteered to give it to him. He in no way wronged me, and I was so happy to give it, so... Still, the irritation persisted.

This is not the only time, I have found myself in the presence of someone that we have helped, wondering why we helped them and not the other way around. But all that comes from our worldly knowledge and sense of equity and fairness. In the kingdom, we are not looking for fairness or equity. The cross was not fair, and our salvation contains no equity. The kingdom is so foreign to our natural understandings that its principals can seem wrong to us. But the kingdom is never unjust, immoral, or unrighteous, we just have to learn to live, walk, and see in its light.

Remember, it's more blessed to give than to receive and, give and it shall be given unto you. (**Acts 20:35 & Luke 6:38**) Well, then the lesser should bless the greater, right? I remember a serious religious debate with a pastor one night at a restaurant about who would pick up the check. I was very young and he was much better off financially than I. I argued to no avail that I should pay because I needed the return blessings all the more.

We should, I should, simply endeavor to be led by His Spirit and desire to be a blessing to any and all we are called to help.

Testify...

Pray...

Prophesy...

For God is working in you, giving you the *desire* and the *power* to do what pleases him.

Philippians 2:13 (NLT)

Week #45

Good Morning, today we will be reading **Genesis 24:34-35** (NASB).

³⁴ So he said, "I am Abraham's servant. ³⁵ The Lord has greatly blessed my master, so that he has become rich; and He has given him flocks and herds, and silver and gold, and servants and maids, and camels and donkeys.

And again Genesis 24:34-35 (NLT)

³⁴ "I am Abraham's servant," he explained. ³⁵ "And the Lord has greatly blessed my master; he has become a wealthy man. The Lord has given him flocks of sheep and goats, herds of cattle, a fortune in silver and gold, and many male and female servants and camels and donkeys.

Let's also look at Abraham's son Isaac... **Genesis 26:12-14** (NKJV)

¹² Then Isaac sowed in that land, and reaped in the same year a hundredfold; and the Lord blessed him. ¹³ The man began to prosper, and continued prospering until he became very prosperous; ¹⁴ for he had possessions of flocks and possessions of herds and a great number of servants. So the Philistines envied him.

And again **Genesis 26:12-14** (NLT)

¹² When Isaac planted his crops that year, he harvested a hundred times more grain than he planted, for the Lord blessed him. ¹³ He became a very rich man, and his wealth continued to grow. ¹⁴ He acquired so many flocks of sheep and goats, herds of cattle, and servants that the Philistines became jealous of him.

So, what happens when you walk with God? What happens when you go where He sends you? What happens when you stay where He has placed you? What happens when you abide in Him?

Defeating kings with your own trained servants... **(Genesis 14:14-16)** Entire nations get nervous about you... **(Genesis 26:16)**

We are walking with **Jehovah Jireh** - the LORD will provide; He will see to it.

Provide what? See to what? All that you will ever need, He is God Almighty, **El Shaddai** – more than enough, more than sufficient.

We pray the Lord bless you, today.

A Testimony....

One summer we volunteered to help with a couple of church upkeep projects. First, I have learned over many years that volunteering is so much better, for all involved than being drafted. And for the sake of our dear pastors, let us always be quick to volunteer anytime the Spirit gives us an open door.

Each project seemed rather straight forward, quick, and simple enough. Well, things are not always as simple as they seem. We were sealing some areas of concrete around the church. The product we were applying was so viscous that it required every ounce of strength I could muster to get it out of the tube. We bent, broke, and incapacitated two caulking guns in the process. It took several trips to the store for better tools and more product, not to mention several hours kneeling on the concrete.

We also painted the church's parking lot stripes. This seemed a simple, easy job in theory, but not so much in real-world application. Some of the lines were so far gone, and much of the concrete was so pitted, that it took gallons and gallons more paint than expected. It was nice and hot, great for the paint to dry, but not so great for those applying the paint. One day it began to rain, refreshing for us, but horrible for the paint we just laid down. The cleaning, clearing, and coat after coat in the hot sun, melted us like butter. It wound up taking us a month of Saturdays to finish the job.

In both cases as soon as I could really see the time and effort each of these projects was going to require, I wanted to call in the professionals. I was more than ready, willing, and able to pay for someone else, anyone else to come finish these jobs. But the Lord had given us our assignments, so we persevered.

Why wouldn't God let me just pay someone to do those jobs? Maybe it was to help in my own patient endurance. Maybe it was to let my children see that the church is worth actual hard work. Maybe it was to let the people in the neighborhood around the church see how much we loved our church. Maybe it was to show the pastor that we would be with him in these endeavors no matter the cost, the effort, or the time. Maybe, just maybe, it was all of the above.

Devoted Money, doesn't have to always and only be about money. Money is just an exchange medium for effort, time, and skill. Sometimes, many times, we can just cut out the middle man. We can give up our time, break our tools, rain down buckets of sweat, and get yellow paint all over our truck bed, just to say we love this Kingdom.

Testify...

Pray...

Prophesy...

This is the heritage of the servants of the Lord, and their righteousness is of me, saith the Lord.

Isaiah 54:17 (KJV)

Week #46

Good Morning, today we will be reading **1 Timothy 6:9-10** (NKJV).

⁹ BUT THOSE WHO DESIRE TO BE RICH FALL INTO TEMPTATION AND A SNARE, AND INTO MANY FOOLISH AND HARMFUL LUSTS WHICH DROWN MEN IN DESTRUCTION AND PERDITION. ¹⁰ FOR THE LOVE OF MONEY IS A ROOT OF ALL KINDS OF EVIL, FOR WHICH SOME HAVE STRAYED FROM THE FAITH IN THEIR GREEDINESS, AND PIERCED THEMSELVES THROUGH WITH MANY SORROWS.

And **1 Timothy 6:9-10** (GNT)

⁹ BUT THOSE WHO WANT TO GET RICH FALL INTO TEMPTATION AND ARE CAUGHT IN THE TRAP OF MANY FOOLISH AND HARMFUL DESIRES, WHICH PULL THEM DOWN TO RUIN AND DESTRUCTION. ¹⁰ FOR THE LOVE OF MONEY IS A SOURCE OF ALL KINDS OF EVIL. SOME HAVE BEEN SO EAGER TO HAVE IT THAT THEY HAVE WANDERED AWAY FROM THE FAITH AND HAVE BROKEN THEIR HEARTS WITH MANY SORROWS.

And again **1 Timothy 6:9-10** (HCSB)

⁹ BUT THOSE WHO WANT TO BE RICH FALL INTO TEMPTATION, A TRAP, AND MANY FOOLISH AND HARMFUL DESIRES, WHICH PLUNGE PEOPLE INTO RUIN AND DESTRUCTION. ¹⁰ FOR THE LOVE OF MONEY IS A ROOT OF ALL KINDS OF EVIL, AND BY CRAVING IT, SOME HAVE WANDERED AWAY FROM THE FAITH AND PIERCED THEMSELVES WITH MANY PAINS.

And finally, **1 Timothy 6:9-10** (NLT)

⁹ BUT PEOPLE WHO LONG TO BE RICH FALL INTO TEMPTATION AND ARE TRAPPED BY MANY FOOLISH AND HARMFUL DESIRES THAT PLUNGE THEM INTO RUIN AND DESTRUCTION. ¹⁰ FOR THE LOVE OF MONEY IS THE ROOT OF ALL KINDS OF EVIL. AND SOME PEOPLE, CRAVING MONEY, HAVE WANDERED FROM THE TRUE FAITH AND PIERCED THEMSELVES WITH MANY SORROWS.

Ok, forgive this silly little question, why do people want to be rich?

Well, doesn't wealth bring security, ease, opportunity, and comfort? Maybe for a season, but why do we want all those things? We are all looking for life. Unfortunately, we have been led down a wrong path, when we think that money brings life and life more abundantly (there is only One who does that). Many, many people (beloved Christians included) chase after money hoping to attain life (a better life). But when we capture that money, we quickly find out that its life is not real Life. Now, the truly insidious thing is that it always cries out that if you only had more, and more, and even more then you would have life. So many keep on chasing and chasing. Money isn't good or evil, but chasing it will never lead to life.

But we know, where life is and who Life is. Our faith knows where real security and opportunity resides. We walk with the Comforter Himself, and abundance is found in Abundant Life Himself (**John 10:10**).

We pray the Lord bless you, today.

A Testimony....

Here is a testimony that I do not want to tell. I can recall two times when I let concern for money really spoil great times and events in my life.

Once was while we lived in Japan. We had paid for the airline tickets to fly over two young men who had been in a youth group I taught back in Oklahoma. It was a great opportunity for them to literally see the other side of the planet. It was great to see them and we went and did many cool things in Japan. But as the visit went on the calculator in my head began to get louder and louder. It tainted what should have been fun, exciting, and beneficial. I do not to this day regret one dollar or one yen spent on their visit. I do regret that concern and anxiousness over money hindered even in subtle and slight ways the full benefit of those days.

The other time was when my family stopped in Hawaii on our way back to the States. I mean, it was pretty much on the way, so we went to Hawaii for a family vacation. Now, it was a good trip and we did many things and enjoyed it very much. But that calculator in my head started running and then ruining a great family adventure. If I could have just rested in Him, and marveled at where He had brought me to, that enjoyment and adventure would have been beyond anything I had seen or known.

So why did I get anxious and concerned about money? Well, to be shockingly, blindingly honest, it is because I let money creep up into a spot in my life where it doesn't belong. When I let money edge its way to the top of the leader board, and presume that it's god in my life, things don't go well. Money is simply a medium of exchange. It does not take care of me, it does not provide for me, and it certainly does not bring me life. I have to always let God be my God, nothing else can assume that role.

I had a friend come to me one time to talk about some financial matters. They had always thought that their family's struggles with money were due to their spending. But now God was showing them it was actually their faith in money and not in Him. The Lord had me share something I had witnessed many years ago. They had bought a power tool and just before the warranty was up, they turned the battery in for a new one because it wouldn't hold a full charge. Now, this wasn't lying, cheating, or stealing, but it wasn't right. They used the tool often, and they knew that the batteries normally hold less charge over time. So, why play that angle? Why take every advantage? In this case, it revealed a hole in their faith. They had to find every loophole because they had to take care of themselves. Which implies... (they actually believed) God would not.

We need to labor to enter into His rest (**Hebrews 4:11**). We need to run to Him. We (I) need to repent (turn around) each time money takes up residence in a place it does not belong. Running to His Word for faith, and His Spirit to change our nature and strengthen our hearts. This is how we choose whom we will serve and who will be our God and our Lord.

Testify...

Pray...

Prophesy...

Surely you know that you are God's temple and that God's Spirit lives in you!

1 Corinthians 3:16 (GNT)

Week #47

Good Morning, today we will be reading **1 Timothy 6:17-19** (KJV).

¹⁷ CHARGE THEM THAT ARE RICH IN THIS WORLD, THAT THEY BE NOT HIGHMINDED, NOR TRUST IN UNCERTAIN RICHES, BUT IN THE LIVING GOD, WHO GIVETH US RICHLY ALL THINGS TO ENJOY; ¹⁸ THAT THEY DO GOOD, THAT THEY BE RICH IN GOOD WORKS, READY TO DISTRIBUTE, WILLING TO COMMUNICATE; ¹⁹ LAYING UP IN STORE FOR THEMSELVES A GOOD FOUNDATION AGAINST THE TIME TO COME, THAT THEY MAY LAY HOLD ON ETERNAL LIFE.

And **1 Timothy 6:17-19** (GW)

¹⁷ TELL THOSE WHO HAVE THE RICHES OF THIS WORLD NOT TO BE ARROGANT AND NOT TO PLACE THEIR CONFIDENCE IN ANYTHING AS UNCERTAIN AS RICHES. INSTEAD, THEY SHOULD PLACE THEIR CONFIDENCE IN GOD WHO RICHLY PROVIDES US WITH EVERYTHING TO ENJOY. ¹⁸ TELL THEM TO DO GOOD, TO DO A LOT OF GOOD THINGS, TO BE GENEROUS, AND TO SHARE. ¹⁹ BY DOING THIS THEY STORE UP A TREASURE FOR THEMSELVES WHICH IS A GOOD FOUNDATION FOR THE FUTURE. IN THIS WAY THEY TAKE HOLD OF WHAT LIFE REALLY IS.

And again **1 Timothy 6:17-19** (HCSB)

¹⁷ INSTRUCT THOSE WHO ARE RICH IN THE PRESENT AGE NOT TO BE ARROGANT OR TO SET THEIR HOPE ON THE UNCERTAINTY OF WEALTH, BUT ON GOD, WHO RICHLY PROVIDES US WITH ALL THINGS TO ENJOY. ¹⁸ INSTRUCT THEM TO DO WHAT IS GOOD, TO BE RICH IN GOOD WORKS, TO BE GENEROUS, WILLING TO SHARE, ¹⁹ STORING UP FOR THEMSELVES A GOOD RESERVE FOR THE AGE TO COME, SO THAT THEY MAY TAKE HOLD OF LIFE THAT IS REAL.

And finally, **1 Timothy 6:17-19** (NLT)

¹⁷ TEACH THOSE WHO ARE RICH IN THIS WORLD NOT TO BE PROUD AND NOT TO TRUST IN THEIR MONEY, WHICH IS SO UNRELIABLE. THEIR TRUST SHOULD BE IN GOD, WHO RICHLY GIVES US ALL WE NEED FOR OUR ENJOYMENT. ¹⁸ TELL THEM TO USE THEIR MONEY TO DO GOOD. THEY SHOULD BE RICH IN GOOD WORKS AND GENEROUS TO THOSE IN NEED, ALWAYS BEING READY TO SHARE WITH OTHERS. ¹⁹ BY DOING THIS THEY WILL BE STORING UP THEIR TREASURE AS A GOOD FOUNDATION FOR THE FUTURE SO THAT THEY MAY EXPERIENCE TRUE LIFE.

God and His Word are not bipolar. He pours out blessings which we cannot contain (riches), and then condemn all those with riches. He wants us blessed and walking in abundance but that abundance (riches) cannot ever have our heart. We have clear instruction just how dangerous that is (**1 Timothy 6:9-10**). We also have clear instruction as to what we should do with these riches (v. 17-19). When we keep our hearts right before God and love people more than money, we can walk in abundance.

We pray the Lord bless you, today.

A Testimony....

As I have told, when my daughter was born I quit my job to stay home with her. After a few years, she started going to my mother's daycare and I went back to work. Then when our family moved to Japan, I again stayed home with my daughter and younger son. As they both grew and Micah started school, I again went back to work. But we could see that for our family it was best if someone stayed home. So, when we moved again back to the States, I didn't go to work but stayed at home.

A decade or so rolled by and soon enough my daughter was driving and my son was in middle school. So, I made plans to go back to work. I wanted to be able to work and save more money for our retirement savings. It would only be a couple of years or so before we retired and move to the farm. I could see that this money would give us a better footing when we retired.

Some months before everything was going to be in place to allow me to go back to work, a change happened. It became quite apparent that my mother-in-law needed to come live near us. She had been living in the home we had in Oklahoma before we moved to Japan. She had retired from her job and was starting to have some health and daily living concerns. We made arrangements and found a senior apartment complex near our home. Even after all was settled it was apparent that I would need to be able to help her with some aspects of her daily life. So, my going back to work would just not be feasible.

It's a whole other testimony about how God worked on my heart. So that when this time came, I could see it not as a *have to*, but a *get to*. She is a daughter of Almighty God, what higher honor could I have but to help her in ways great and small.

Now, what about that money I had planned on making? Well the house she was moving out of, was on the other side of the state from our farm. We didn't need it anymore, and it would be a terrible hassle to try to maintain it and rent it from so far away.

It was also in some disarray and disrepair since we had been living so far away for so long. So, we put the home up for sale at a very reasonable price. We found a young man, who was excited to own the home and put in the work to restore it. We settled everything and guess what numbers lined right up? We had sold the house for just slightly more than I was projected to earn over the few years of working. I clearly heard my Father, He had me covered and I was free to care for His daughter.

Testify...

Pray...

Prophesy...

²⁸ For thou wilt light my candle: the LORD my God will enlighten my darkness.
²⁹ For by thee I have run through a troop; and by my God have I leaped over a wall.
³⁰ As for God, his way is perfect: the word of the LORD is tried: he is a buckler to all those that trust in him.
³¹ For who is God save the LORD? or who is a rock save our God?
³² It is God that girdeth me with strength, and maketh my way perfect.
³³ He maketh my feet like hinds' feet, and setteth me upon my high places.
³⁴ He teacheth my hands to war, so that a bow of steel is broken by mine arms.
³⁵ Thou hast also given me the shield of thy salvation: and thy right hand hath holden me up, and thy gentleness hath made me great.
³⁶ Thou hast enlarged my steps under me, that my feet did not slip.

Psalms 18:28-36 (KJV)

Week #48

Good Morning, today we will be reading **Genesis 32:10** (NLT).

I AM NOT WORTHY OF ALL THE UNFAILING LOVE AND FAITHFULNESS YOU HAVE SHOWN TO ME, YOUR SERVANT. WHEN I LEFT HOME AND CROSSED THE JORDAN RIVER, I OWNED NOTHING EXCEPT A WALKING STICK. NOW MY HOUSEHOLD FILLS TWO LARGE CAMPS!

And Genesis 36:6-7 (GNT)

⁶ THEN ESAU TOOK HIS WIVES, HIS SONS, HIS DAUGHTERS, AND ALL THE PEOPLE OF HIS HOUSE, ALONG WITH ALL HIS LIVESTOCK AND ALL THE POSSESSIONS HE HAD GOTTEN IN THE LAND OF CANAAN, AND WENT AWAY FROM HIS BROTHER JACOB TO ANOTHER LAND. ⁷ HE LEFT BECAUSE THE LAND WHERE HE AND JACOB WERE LIVING WAS NOT ABLE TO SUPPORT THEM; THEY HAD TOO MUCH LIVESTOCK AND COULD NO LONGER STAY TOGETHER.

And Genesis 39:20 (NASB)

SO JOSEPH'S MASTER TOOK HIM AND PUT HIM INTO THE JAIL, THE PLACE WHERE THE KING'S PRISONERS WERE CONFINED; AND HE WAS THERE IN THE JAIL.

And Genesis 41:38-44 (NASB)

³⁸ THEN PHARAOH SAID TO HIS SERVANTS, "CAN WE FIND A MAN LIKE THIS, IN WHOM IS A DIVINE SPIRIT?" ³⁹ SO PHARAOH SAID TO JOSEPH, "SINCE GOD HAS INFORMED YOU OF ALL THIS, THERE IS NO ONE SO DISCERNING AND WISE AS YOU ARE. ⁴⁰ YOU SHALL BE OVER MY HOUSE, AND ACCORDING TO YOUR COMMAND ALL MY PEOPLE SHALL DO HOMAGE; ONLY IN THE THRONE I WILL BE GREATER THAN YOU." ⁴¹ PHARAOH SAID TO JOSEPH, "SEE, I HAVE SET YOU OVER ALL THE LAND OF EGYPT." ⁴² THEN PHARAOH TOOK OFF HIS SIGNET RING FROM HIS HAND AND PUT IT ON JOSEPH'S HAND, AND CLOTHED HIM IN GARMENTS OF FINE LINEN AND PUT THE GOLD NECKLACE AROUND HIS NECK. ⁴³ HE HAD HIM RIDE IN HIS SECOND CHARIOT; AND THEY PROCLAIMED BEFORE HIM, "BOW THE KNEE!" AND HE SET HIM OVER ALL THE LAND OF EGYPT. ⁴⁴ MOREOVER, PHARAOH SAID TO JOSEPH, "THOUGH I AM PHARAOH, YET WITHOUT YOUR PERMISSION NO ONE SHALL RAISE HIS HAND OR FOOT IN ALL THE LAND OF EGYPT."

Both Israel (formerly known as Jacob) and Joseph grew up in very wealthy homes. Each one of them came to a point where they had nothing. But God... But the blessing of God...

God is blessing; it is not only His nature, it is Him. He flows from Him, abounding and overflowing. It will change even the worst circumstances that we could ever find ourselves in. We simply have to learn not to resist it, not to resist Him. Remember **El Shaddai**, more than enough, that means there will be too much. What shall we ever do with all that too much? Feed the hungry, clothe the naked, house the homeless, and preach the Good News to all the world. Ready, Set, Go...

We pray the Lord bless you, today.

A Testimony....
   I want to share my testimony on budgets, but first I want to share a little something very precious to me. I can remember when I got out on my own. The Lord was so gracious and kind to me, even back when my heart was in dire need of an overhaul. I remember getting to the point where I had extra dollars each week. This was the height of riches for me. I could just pop into a convenience store and by a fountain drink. No stress, no rearranging the budget, and no condemnation of spending that 99cents on such a frivolous thing. I had found wealth and riches; I had more than enough.
   Then as time rolled by the Lord brought me to a place where I had tens of dollars extra each week. Well, that was just decadence. I could go actually shopping for things I wanted, not just for the things I needed. Well, life can't get better than that, can it? God is the God of more... So, soon enough He brought me to the land of extra hundreds and quickly thereafter extra thousands. In this place, we really have to take our eyes off ourselves. This money is in no way all for us. Lord, show us who this money is for. Who can we bless, how can we help? That next wrung on this ladder could never happen to me and my family, right? We just don't make that kind of money... God is not limited by us, our salary, our culture, or our nationality. But surely that one with 5 zeros is simply out of the question, I mean... God even took us to that place, and we used those 5 zeros to buy our farm. We have to find the faith, not to limit Him.
   Ok, budgets. I am a numbers kind of a person. I have been educated in such things, and I enjoy the cold, definite, precision of mathematics. So, for decades I made budgets for my family. I do believe this was a good step for me to take on my walk with God. But it is just so hard to contain God and His blessings. You just can't make His overflowing abundance fit into a spreadsheet. He nearly constantly wrecked my budgets. First, He would have us give away an unexpected amount. So, we would go to adjust the budget accordingly, but then there would be more money. We live on an almost entirely set income. I should be able to plan and budget for the next decade, but God... So, eventually, I gave up on my budgets and simply endeavor to just walk with Him and be led by His Spirit.
   But with a few years to go until retirement, my wife seemed to grow more inquisitive about our finances. So, I made a budget and projected it out into retirement. I warned her that God would mess with these numbers. And within 24hrs there was another $9,000 and within two weeks another $3,400. It was a joy to share these things with her. She could see right there on the spreadsheet, God interfering with our money and wrecking our budgets. I still to this day do not understand His math. He subtracts from our budgets (when He calls us to give extra) and we wind up with even more. He adds and multiplies by first subtracting. Well, as for my house we simply bow, He is God and His math is higher than our math. All glory to God.

Testify...

Pray...

Prophesy...

Do you have the gift of speaking? Then speak as though God himself were speaking through you. Do you have the gift of helping others? Do it with all the strength and energy that God supplies. Then everything you do will bring glory to God through Jesus Christ. All glory and power to him forever and ever! Amen.

1 Peter 4:11 (NLT)

Week #49

Good Morning, today we will be reading **Matthew 16:24-27** (NKJV).

²⁴ Then Jesus said to His disciples, "If anyone desires to come after Me, let him deny himself, and take up his cross, and follow Me. ²⁵ For whoever desires to save his life will lose it, but whoever loses his life for My sake will find it. ²⁶ For what profit is it to a man if he gains the whole world, and loses his own soul? Or what will a man give in exchange for his soul? ²⁷ For the Son of Man will come in the glory of His Father with His angels, and then He will reward each according to his works.

And **Matthew 16:24-27** (NLT)

²⁴ Then Jesus said to his disciples, "If any of you wants to be my follower, you must give up your own way, take up your cross, and follow me. ²⁵ If you try to hang on to your life, you will lose it. But if you give up your life for my sake, you will save it. ²⁶ And what do you benefit if you gain the whole world but lose your own soul? Is anything worth more than your soul? ²⁷ For the Son of Man will come with his angels in the glory of his Father and will judge all people according to their deeds. ²⁸ And I tell you the truth, some standing here right now will not die before they see the Son of Man coming in his Kingdom."

Remember **Matthew 6:24** (NLT)

²⁴ "No one can serve two masters. For you will hate one and love the other; you will be devoted to one and despise the other. You cannot serve God and be enslaved to money.

Do we believe Him? Can we trust in Him and His ways? Can we let go of our life and trust that it will be ok? Do we know, He is Life?

Remember **Hebrews 11:6** (NKJV)

But without faith it is impossible to please Him, for he who comes to God must believe that He is, and that He is a rewarder of those who diligently seek Him.

And then we must choose, **Joshua 24:15** (NKJV)

¹⁵ And if it seems evil to you to serve the Lord, choose for yourselves this day whom you will serve, whether the gods which your fathers served that were on the other side of the River, or the gods of the Amorites, in whose land you dwell. But as for me and my house, we will serve the Lord."

We pray the Lord bless you, today.

A Testimony….

I can remember standing in an entrance to a church that I attended and looking down at bricks that had been engraved with names. These were the names of the people who gave to support the building of this church. I only recognized a hand full of those names. Some of those people had moved away, some had gone on to other works in the Kingdom, and some had gone home to be with our Lord. But those bricks have stuck with me over some twenty years. Even though most of those people have gone on, in one way or another, their work there at that church still continued.

This combined with my lessons learned from my slothfulness and lack of faith concerning the support of that Baltic states church project (Week#15) has made me zealous concerning church building projects. What a great investment in the Kingdom. It may continue to bless people long after we have left this world. I believe these opportunities should be cherished and sought after. We should use our money wisely, and let it work to build those heavenly treasures.

Remember that rather strange parable Jesus told of the shrewd manager (**Luke 16:1-9**). He used his dealings with money to make a way for himself. Jesus said the world is shrewder when using their money than the children of God. We need to turn that around, don't we? We need to, "use worldly wealth." We should use it to help others, build the Kingdom, and lay up an abundance of that eternal wealth.

So, when my pastor announced one Sunday morning that the church needed new front doors, I was excited, to say the least. I wanted to jump right up and say, "Done!" But I didn't want to be selfish and deny my brothers and sisters the opportunity to participate. So, I held off. I wanted to make up any gap between what was received in the offering and what was needed. But that was going to require waiting for all the accounting to settle. It just wasn't in my heart to wait. So, we just wrote the check out to pay for the doors, $700. Let the church figure out what to do with the extra. We should be constantly giving this kind of trouble to the accountant and the pastor.

I love to see those doors to this day. I love to see people enter that church through those doors. What a wonderful kingdom God has made. He allows us to participate in His Kingdom. Showing our deep love and appreciation for Him, His Kingdom, and His people with our giving.

Testify...

Pray...

Prophesy...

Love has been perfected among us in this: that we may have boldness in the day of judgment; because as He is, so are we in this world.

1 John 4:17 (NKJV)

Week #50

Good Morning, today we will be reading **Luke 17:30-33** (NKJV).

³⁰ Even so will it be in the day when the Son of Man is revealed. ³¹ "In that day, he who is on the housetop, and his goods are in the house, let him not come down to take them away. And likewise the one who is in the field, let him not turn back. ³² Remember Lot's wife. ³³ Whoever seeks to save his life will lose it, and whoever loses his life will preserve it.

And Luke 17:30-33 (NLT)

³⁰ Yes, it will be 'business as usual' right up to the day when the Son of Man is revealed. ³¹ On that day a person out on the deck of a roof must not go down into the house to pack. A person out in the field must not return home. ³² Remember what happened to Lot's wife! ³³ If you cling to your life, you will lose it, and if you let your life go, you will save it.

Obviously, these scriptures are referring to the return of Christ. The question that they bring up is where will your attention be on that day. Where will our eyes look to when He splits that eastern sky. Will we look back on our dream home, our classic car, our silver and gold, those family heirlooms, or those European antiques. Surely, we would not look back on that giant flat screen tv or that comfy leather recliner. Are we not so in love with our Savior that none of these things will matter when He appears? And if they won't matter then, how can they matter now. If they won't have our hearts then, they shouldn't have our hearts now.

Didn't we give up our lives when we came to Christ? Remember going under that water at baptism? Didn't we realize how empty, shallow, meaningless our wreck of an existence was? Isn't that why we ran to our Savior, to save us? How could we look back? What about those Israelites? Did they look back? How could they want to go back, after they had been saved and delivered?

How about the rich young ruler (**Mark 10:17-22**)? What would you give up for an opportunity to walk with Jesus? It will cost you everything. But that is not the end of the story. Once our heart is right and our walk set...

Then **Mark 10:28-31** (NKJV)

²⁸ Then Peter began to say to Him, "See, we have left all and followed You." ²⁹ So Jesus answered and said, "Assuredly, I say to you, there is no one who has left house or brothers or sisters or father or mother or wife or children or lands, for My sake and the gospel's, ³⁰ who shall not receive a hundredfold now in this time—houses and brothers and sisters and mothers and children and lands, with persecutions—and in the age to come, eternal life. ³¹ But many *who are* first will be last, and the last first."

We pray the Lord bless you, today.

A Testimony....

The last three of these testimonies are really just one big one, broken into three parts. This is the progression that God has brought me through in my understanding of His Kingdom.

When God gave me my new heart, I was so happy to participate in the Kingdom. One pastor who went over to Russia has always been near my heart. I have always been overjoyed to give towards his ministry. I am usually in shock and can't find words to speak when his staff will periodically call and thank our family for our support. I really should be thanking him. Through him, I get to minister in Russia and all it cost me is money. He left everything and went to another, other side of the planet.

Now we weren't able to give any massive amounts but we remained steady in our giving. I always kind of wondered about our *return on investment*. I would wonder what it actually costs him to run his entire ministry. See, if I knew that then I could calculate my percentage and then get to see my return. I was excited to be a part, and I was elated to do my part would lead to a share of the rewards. If I gave $20/month and their budget was $20,000/month then I have a 1/1000 share. So if 1,000 people get saved that month, I get credit for one, right?

I even began to look for other ministries. Investing in ministries that fed the hungry, gave shelter to the homeless, visited those in prison. Those that help the young and the old. Those that preached the gospel, in word and in deed. I want to use my money wisely and bless my dearly loved Savior. Remember, **Matthew 25:34-36** (NKJV).

³⁴ Then the King will say to those on His right hand, 'Come, you blessed of My Father, inherit the kingdom prepared for you from the foundation of the world: ³⁵ for I was hungry and you gave Me food; I was thirsty and you gave Me drink; I was a stranger and you took Me in; ³⁶ I was naked and you clothed Me; I was sick and you visited Me; I was in prison and you came to Me.'

I was actively participating in the kingdom and excited to do so. I could also see far out into eternity and see the heavenly returns of these investments. All those people helped and blessed, surely, we would rejoice together in the Goodness of God for eternity.

But my understanding of the Kingdom was limited by what I could receive and process. It took some years for God to grow, develop, and stretch me enough; so that we could have a little conversation...

To Be Continued –

Testify...

_____
_____
_____
_____
_____
_____
_____

Pray...

_____
_____
_____
_____
_____
_____
_____

Prophesy...

_____
_____
_____
_____
_____

Finally, there is laid up for me the crown of righteousness, which the Lord, the righteous Judge, will give to me on that Day, and not to me only but also to all who have loved His appearing.

2 Timothy 4:8 (NKJV)

Week #51

Good Morning, today we will be reading **Titus 3:13-14** (NKJV).
¹³ Send Zenas the lawyer and Apollos on their journey with haste, that they may lack nothing. ¹⁴ And let our people also learn to maintain good works, to meet urgent needs, that they may not be unfruitful.

And **Titus 3:13-14** (NLT)
¹³ Do everything you can to help Zenas the lawyer and Apollos with their trip. See that they are given everything they need. ¹⁴ Our people must learn to do good by meeting the urgent needs of others; then they will not be unproductive.

And finally, **Titus 3:13-14** (GNT)
¹³ Do your best to help Zenas the lawyer and Apollos to get started on their travels, and see to it that they have everything they need. ¹⁴ Our people must learn to spend their time doing good, in order to provide for real needs; they should not live useless lives.

We must learn to do good through our giving, meeting the urgent needs people have in this world, in which we now walk. Do we see this as a great opportunity? Or, do we get imbittered toward God when He calls on us to give? I sure used to... But God will deliver us from that self-centered life and ignite our faith through love.

Our giving does not increase God's blessing over us. Our giving simply reveals our faith. Our giving shows when we really trust Him to provide and care for us. And that faith is our access to all His blessings. Our faith in Jesus and His completed work on the cross is our access to everything God has for us (in Him all the promises are, "Yes" and, "Amen" – **1 Corinthians 1:20**). Let that faith in His work permeate your whole life including your finances. Then literally try not to get in the way. The blessing of God is upon you because of Jesus. Receive it, and be blessed. Now that you have received the blessing of God, you are well taken care of both here and now, and throughout eternity. Now, you are free. Free from concerns about me, myself, and I. Now, you, me, we, and I can set to our real work, helping others. We can be generous because God has us. He will not slumber nor sleep. He has the power, ability, and the will to bless and keep us. When we remember our two commandments – Love God, love your neighbor as yourself – money will find its proper place. We will be free, free to walk with Him and be led by His Spirit into all these good works.

We pray the Lord bless you, today.

A Testimony....

I had my understanding of participating in the Kingdom and receiving a partial share based on how much I had helped. I thought this was the height of the Goodness of God, that He made a way for us to join together. That He made a way for us to work together and benefit together. Then God wanted to have a little talk...

The Lord came to me and challenged my percentage understanding and my division of the rewards. He told me that my reward was not 1 of those 1,000 saved, but all of them. What? Wait, a minute. That can't be... That's not right. That's not fair. It's amazing to me the closer we get to understanding God and His Kingdom, the more phrases like "not right" and "not fair" pop up. How about salvation through Jesus's sacrifice? How about seated together with Him, and as He is so are we? Fair?

It just could not be that I would get an equal share with those that did so much more than me. God then asked me, "Did you do what I gave you to do?" Well, yes. But, how could... I was at a loss for words, this really took a long time to settle in me. God kept leading me along, showing me His nature, and giving me His Word. Like **1 Samuel 30:24** (HCSB)

24 Who can agree to your proposal? The share of the one who goes into battle is to be the same as the share of the one who remains with the supplies. They will share equally." 25 And it has been so from that day forward. David established this policy as a law and an ordinance for Israel and it continues to this very day.

Ok, but doesn't that prove my original point in a share of the reward? The Lord kept bringing it up, the same share, or equal reward. Then the Lord asked me how many souls won to Christ should that minister get credit for? The minister who gave up his whole life. The one who moved his whole family to another nation. The one who had to navigate new languages, new traditions, new customs, and a whole new governmental system. What was the right percentage for him to receive? Well, I spoke right up loud and clear. He should get credit for each and every soul won to Christ. (The whole 1,000 in our example.)

Then the Lord had me. I walked right into that one. Well, it's not like I was going to win the argument anyway, but still. The Lord said, that was a good and right judgment; now, your share has to be equal to his... But it seems so unfair, so beyond good, and above all, I could ask or think.

The Lord showed me a beautiful picture, all of us working together. Using our giftings and obeying our callings, and all of us sharing the fruit of those labors equally.

Still, God was not done showing me the full extent of the Goodness of His Kingdom. He let me mediate and settle this step in my understanding, and then some years later we had another talk...

To Be Continued –

Testify...

Pray...

Prophesy...

but grow in the grace and knowledge of our Lord and Savior Jesus Christ. To Him be the glory both now and forever. Amen.

2 Peter 3:18 *(NKJV)*

Week #52

Good Morning, today we will be reading **Philippians 4:15-17** (NASB).
¹⁵ You yourselves also know, Philippians, that at the first preaching of the gospel, after I left Macedonia, no church shared with me in the matter of giving and receiving but you alone; ¹⁶ for even in Thessalonica you sent a gift more than once for my needs. ¹⁷ Not that I seek the gift itself, but I seek for the profit which increases to your account. ¹⁸ But I have received everything in full and have an abundance; I am amply supplied, having received from Epaphroditus what you have sent, a fragrant aroma, an acceptable sacrifice, well-pleasing to God. ¹⁹ And my God will supply all your needs according to His riches in glory in Christ Jesus. ²⁰ Now to our God and Father be the glory forever and ever. Amen.

You just can't stop those Philippians from giving. It's in their heart, they loved Paul. They wanted to bless the kingdom and people. When our heart is right, giving is such a joy, you really just don't want to stop.

And **James 2:14-17** (KJV)
¹⁴ What doth it profit, my brethren, though a man say he hath faith, and have not works? Can faith save him?
¹⁵ If a brother or sister be naked, and destitute of daily food,
¹⁶ And one of you say unto them, Depart in peace, be ye warmed and filled; notwithstanding ye give them not those things which are needful to the body; what doth it profit?
¹⁷ Even so faith, if it hath not works, is dead, being alone.

Faith inspires, compels, and demands action, faith without action just isn't faith. Faith is knowing and seeing something that cannot be known or seen in this present world. We know that He is God, He is Good, and He is actively caring for us. We are settled and complete by faith, even when it does not appear that way in this present world. Now we are free to focus on others... Now, we give... and give our life away.

Faith just can't be stopped when it's powered by Love. When we know God loves us, we begin to rest and trust in Him. When we are not so sure whether He loves us or is mad at us, our faith can falter. When we wonder what God will do for us, or what He may do to us, our love has not yet been perfected (**1 John 4:18**). Let us be emboldened by the Love our God has for us. He has saved us, has He not? **John 3:16-17**, we *know* that one right? He *so* loves us. And now that the Almighty loves us, what do we have to fear? What concern, worry, or anxious thought can abide in our presence? When our love is developed, our faith will be immovable and we shall do mighty exploits.

We pray the Lord bless you, today.

A Testimony....

I was so barely able to handle the Goodness of what God had shown me about His Kingdom. Just being allowed to participate is a sweet kindness from our Father. And allowing us to reap partial rewards would have been, to me, the height of Goodness. But oh, how God's Goodness smashed through all my conceptions of Goodness. To lay a full measure of blessing and reward upon those of us who have participated in such seemingly minor ways, God you are Good. Too Good? Well, of course not, but too good for my understanding, and comprehension. If it were not for the enabling power of your Spirit, I could in no way receive such things.

Ok, but that's it, right? That is as Good as the Goodness of God gets, right? Well, an infinite God who is Good, must have infinite Goodness. So, one day God came to have another talk with me right in the middle of a basketball game.

God showed me a person shooting and making a jump shot. Then He asked me, "Who gets credit for that?" I responded that player, the one who shot the ball. He then asked, "Which part?" Ok, well his hand, his wrist, and his arm. But none of that happens without the brain sending signals via all those nerve cells. And the brain needs the input from the eyes to get the right information to process. The feet, ankles, and legs propelled that jump part of the jump shot, so they get credit. The inner ear allows for proper balance. The lungs provide the oxygen for the muscles, and the heart pumps the blood that delivers it, they get credit. The digestive and endocrine systems certainly play a huge role in the whole process. What about those sweat glands cooling everything down, and that big toe initiating lift off? Well, the longer and longer I processed this question the more the answer became very apparent. The whole body gets the credit for making that basket, not just some part or piece.

He had me again. Again, I just walked right into it. I could see it but it was just too, too Good. If you are in the body, if you are doing your assigned role, then you get credit for what the body does. No matter whether your role is flashy and noticeable, or you're just a big toe; you get credit. It is so, so Good that it nearly brings me to tears to this day. We are the Body of Christ and members in particular.

We get the full blessing and credit for all that the body does. God let me see the reward for my $20 gift did not garner that partial, 1 of a 1,000 reward, nor did it entitle the full 1,000 reward, but it opened the rewards for all that the Body of Christ was doing over this entire planet. See, I told you it was too good. If we were not children of our Father, we would be inclined to use that word, unbelievable.

I know I could never convince you of this, so I will leave it for you to discuss with your Father. I'll leave the room, but I will give one little warning... When you start this conversation with Him, do you really think this is the end of His Goodness?

Remember the parable in **Matthew 20:1-16**. Remember those servants got the same rewards, those who seemed to do little and those that appeared to do much. Some there sure didn't think it was fair. I have this deep stirring that there is so much more that we need to grow into.

> [15] IS IT NOT LAWFUL FOR ME TO DO WHAT I WISH WITH WHAT IS MY OWN? OR IS YOUR EYE ENVIOUS BECAUSE I AM GENEROUS?' [16] SO THE LAST SHALL BE FIRST, AND THE FIRST LAST."
> **Matthew 20:15-16** (NASB)

The work will not be completed without the whole body, so the whole body will share in the rewards for the entire work. Would we want it any other way? Would we want more than some and less than others, when all the grace, power, ability, strength, and will ultimately came from Him, His Son, and His Spirit?

We are one in Him, by Him, through Him, and most certainly because of Him.

You know what we are going to do with those crowns, right?

Revelation 4:10

Testify…

Pray...

Prophesy...

⁶ This poor man cried, and the LORD heard him
And saved him out of all his troubles.
⁷ The angel of the LORD encamps around those who fear Him,
And rescues them.
⁸ O taste and see that the LORD is good;
How blessed is the man who takes refuge in Him!
⁹ O fear the LORD, you His saints;
For to those who fear Him there is no want.
¹⁰ The young lions do lack and suffer hunger;
But they who seek the LORD shall not be in want of any good thing.

Psalms 34:6-10 (NASB)

A parting prayer for all who crossed these pages –

¹⁴ For this reason I bow my knees to the Father of our Lord Jesus Christ, ¹⁵ from whom the whole family in heaven and earth is named, ¹⁶ that He would grant you, according to the riches of His glory, to be strengthened with might through His Spirit in the inner man, ¹⁷ that Christ may dwell in your hearts through faith; that you, being rooted and grounded in love, ¹⁸ may be able to comprehend with all the saints what is the width and length and depth and height— ¹⁹ to know the love of Christ which passes knowledge; that you may be filled with all the fullness of God.

²⁰ Now to Him who is able to do exceedingly abundantly above all that we ask or think, according to the power that works in us, ²¹ to Him be glory in the church by Christ Jesus to all generations, forever and ever. Amen.

Ephesians 3:14-21 (NKJV)

The Heart of the Matter,

We must not settle, we must not be lulled to sleep, and we must push and press; not for our own sake, but for theirs.

We are called to feed the hungry, clothe the naked, care for the elderly. This is the call of God on us, the church. We cannot pass this responsibility over to anyone or anything else. The world ought to know us by our love, and that love should be actively demonstrated as we care and provide for those in need.

They *will* know us by our love one for another. How shall we show this love? In prayers, in fellowships, in kindnesses, in giving and receiving; yes, yes, yes and yes.

³⁵ BY THIS ALL WILL KNOW THAT YOU ARE MY DISCIPLES, IF YOU HAVE LOVE FOR ONE ANOTHER."

John 13:35 (NKJV)

In our giving of ourselves for another, in any and all ways in which that may benefit others, we love.

⁴ LOVE SUFFERS LONG AND IS KIND; LOVE DOES NOT ENVY; LOVE DOES NOT PARADE ITSELF, IS NOT PUFFED UP; ⁵ DOES NOT BEHAVE RUDELY, DOES NOT SEEK ITS OWN, IS NOT PROVOKED, THINKS NO EVIL; ⁶ DOES NOT REJOICE IN INIQUITY, BUT REJOICES IN THE TRUTH; ⁷ BEARS ALL THINGS, BELIEVES ALL THINGS, HOPES ALL THINGS, ENDURES ALL THINGS.

⁸ LOVE NEVER FAILS.

1 Corinthians 13:4-8a (NKJV)

Love ignites our faith
Love inspires our hope
Love steadies our trust
Love propels our giving

Addendum – remember that first love.

Remember being enraptured by love. Whether it was the love for your spouse, the love for your newborn child, or the love for your Savior when He first washed all those sins away. What would we have given for our beloved? Anything? Everything? If we would just let love enrapture us, giving would never be an arduous chore (restraining our giving may become the most difficult of tasks). Enraptured in Love, and led by the Spirit of God, this is the way to life in full abundance.

³ Do nothing out of selfish ambition or vain conceit. Rather, in humility value others above yourselves, ⁴ not looking to your own interests but each of you to the interests of the others.

⁵ In your relationships with one another, have the same mindset as Christ Jesus:

⁶ Who, being in very nature God,
did not consider equality with God something
to be used to his own advantage;
⁷ rather, he made himself nothing
by taking the very nature of a servant,
being made in human likeness.
⁸ And being found in appearance as a man,
he humbled himself
by becoming obedient to death—
even death on a cross!

⁹ Therefore God exalted him to the highest place and gave him the name that is above every name, ¹⁰ that at the name of Jesus every knee should bow, in heaven and on earth and under the earth, ¹¹ and every tongue acknowledge that Jesus Christ is Lord, to the glory of God the Father.

Philippians 2:3-11 (NIV)

Our Hope and Salvation,

    This book was written to and for the believers. But for any and all who may cross these pages and have not found their way home to God through the Salvation of His Son, let me walk you down this wonderful little path home. Jesus is God. Jesus was sent by the Father and became a man, born of a virgin. He walked among us, He taught us, and He did many great miracles. Then He showed us the love of God in suffering on the cross and dying for our sins. When our debts were paid, then the Father sent the Spirit to raise Jesus the Christ from the dead. Jesus destroyed all the works of the enemy and paid for our redemption. We can now be clean, we can now be whole, and we can now be free from sin, death, hell, and the grave. Our forgiveness is just waiting for us to receive it.

IF WE CONFESS OUR SINS, HE IS FAITHFUL AND JUST TO FORGIVE US OUR SINS AND TO CLEANSE US FROM ALL UNRIGHTEOUSNESS.
                                                              1 John 1:9 (NKJV)

    We run to our savior, and we confess our sin. We turn from our own way and our own efforts. We declare that God is our God and that Jesus is our Lord. We trust Him to lead us, protect us, bless us, to remake our nature, and present us to Himself as good Sons and Daughters.

    All this can be heard as we call out His name. All this, is our heart's cry to Him. All our anguish over what we are and what we have done can be heard loud and clear. All our hope and trust that He can fix it all. All our faith that He will not fail to restore, remake, and rebuild all we have lost and destroyed. We know that He will send His Spirit to heal the wounded, wipe away the tears, remove the scars, and perfect the imperfect.

So we cry out, the name, that wonderful name, the powerful name, the name above all other names, and the only name wherein which man might be saved.

Jesus,
Jesus, our savior
Jesus, our Lord
Jesus, my Lord and my God

FOR "WHOEVER CALLS ON THE NAME OF THE LORD SHALL BE SAVED."
ROMANS 10:13 (NKJV)

Jesus

Made in the USA
Columbia, SC
11 September 2020